Power Teams Beyond Borders

Power Teams Beyond Borders

How to Work Remotely and Build Powerful Virtual Teams

Peter Ivanov

WILEY

Library of Congress Cataloging-in-Publication Data is Available:

ISBN 9781119762942 (hardback)
ISBN 9781119763000 (ebk)
ISBN 9781119762997 (ebk)

Cover Design: Wiley
Cover Image: Peter Ivanov

Set in 12/15pt and JansonTextLTStd by SPi Global, Chennai, India

Printed and bound by CPI Group (UK) Ltd, Croydon, CR0 4YY

10 9 8 7 6 5 4 3 2 1

I dedicate this book to my daughters Raina, Sophia, Gergana, Elena and Maia and to all the children in the world whose future depends on the decisions, dedication and commitments we make today. By uniting global talents we can resolve the toughest challenges of humanity.

Contents

Introduction

I want to start by reminding you of five words, which nearly 50 years ago, cast the world simultaneously into fear and hope, and which are still a symbol of the unexpected that calls for urgent action. For three men and their families, these five words meant a one-week life-or-death struggle. These words are: 'Houston, we have a problem.'

Think back to 1970, which incidentally was the year of my birth. It's 11 April and the clock in Houston shows precisely 13:30. It's at this moment that the American space agency NASA shoots the spaceship *Apollo 13* into orbit, with the aim of landing on the moon in four days' time.

On 13 April, there is a loud crash and the three astronauts look out to see a plume of white as their oxygen flows out into space. The two oxygen tanks in the service module have just exploded. The initial reaction back in Houston is one of panic – no one has planned for such a disaster. The families of the three astronauts are horrified. If you've seen the film *Apollo 13* you might remember that at this point in the mission, the spaceship is getting close to the moon. If they continue to fly according to their original plan, they won't have enough energy to reach the gravity of Earth and therefore return to the Earth's surface.

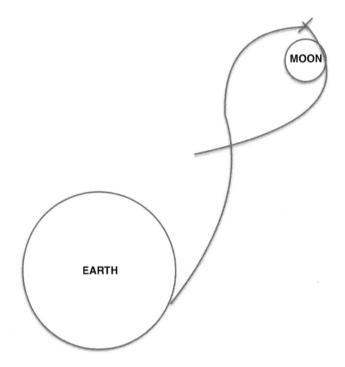

It's now clear that the mission to land on the moon has failed and all of their planned lunar research has been blown away. The focus now is on the lives of the three astronauts. This is a matter of life and death.

Back in Houston, it's 37-year-old Gene Kranz who is in charge at Mission Control when the fateful call from the astronauts comes in. Kranz quickly realises that to save the astronauts' lives, he has to win one fight: the fight for energy.

In space, energy is everything. You need it to move the spaceship, to navigate, to communicate with Mission Control and, of course, to sustain life. At this point, every single unit of energy now means the difference between life and death. They need a miracle.

What does Kranz do in this historic moment? He gathers his whole Houston team into one room. The tension and nervousness is palpable. He lays out the challenge. Brains go into overdrive. Ideas rush around. Everyone's hearts are full with care, fear and hope. Kranz listens carefully to each and every idea being put forward.

Eventually he calls for silence. Then he pulls everyone together – and not just the team in the room with him. He has the three astronauts and hundreds of scientists and engineers from across NASA listening as he calmly says:

> **'We haven't lost a man in space until now and as long as I'm responsible, we won't. Failure is not an option.'**

The seven days of the *Apollo 13* mission were filled with incredible strength of character, flashes of genius, feats of engineering and, above all, an extraterrestrial triumph of leadership.

As we all know, Kranz and his team succeeded in safely bringing the *Apollo 13* astronauts home. But what Kranz also did was succeed in pulling together all these people spread around space, through the magical gravity force of one of the strongest virtual teams the world has ever seen; one whose goal was aligned to one purpose only, to save the lives of the three astronauts on the spaceship.

On 17 April, *Apollo 13* landed, or rather splashed, back to Earth with the command unit carrying the three astronauts landing safely in the Pacific Ocean. The rescue was hailed as a miracle. This is a virtual power team at work.

You might be thinking that the *Apollo 13* was an exceptional case and not one that has applications in general business. But how many of you have worked on a project which has experienced an unexpected change? How often is the budget reduced but you still have to deliver? How often is the go-live date brought forward? How often do team members spread across different locations lose motivation, resulting in a deterioration in the team's performance?

Personally, I've heard the statement, 'Houston, we have a problem' more than once in my career, although thankfully never in relation to a life-or-death situation. But for the projects I was working on, it was critical.

How I Learned to Develop Virtual Power Teams

In the last 25 years, I've had the opportunity to live and work all over Europe. I began my career as a data analyst and have worked across many areas of technology, leading a number of large, multinational virtual teams. Most recently, I was the head of IT services for Eastern Europe, the Middle East and Africa, where I built and led a large team spread across various countries, time zones and from very different cultures.

Through this experience, and if I'm honest mostly from my mistakes, I've developed a highly effective method for creating and leading virtual power teams. But in recent years I started questioning my mission and exploring how I could use my talents to change the world for the better. This was when I decided to leave the worlds of IT and mathematics behind and pursue my dream of becoming an inspirational speaker and coach, focusing on uniting people despite distance. It's this passion that has resulted in this book, where I'm sharing my passion for and knowledge of building virtual power teams.

I like to think of virtual power teams as atoms. You have the nucleus in the centre and then the various particles orbiting that nucleus. In a virtual team, you're building an atom. Your individual team members are the particles and you need to keep them around the nucleus, despite the physical distance between individuals.

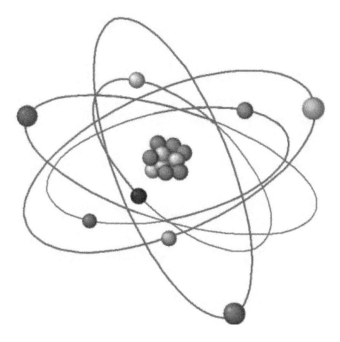

I'll let you into a secret now. The nucleus of this power team isn't the manager or the boss, it isn't any member of the team. It is the purpose and goal of the team that acts as the nucleus, constantly pulling everyone back together.

In this book, I'll explain how to set this goal in such a way that it's aligned with the individual goals and strengths of your team members, while aligning with the overarching purpose and vision of the team. I'll also give you effective tools to put this vital nucleus in place.

2020: The Tipping Point for Global Change?

Globalisation and digital transformation have introduced new challenges in leadership and communication. Teams and projects are often decentralised, crossing international borders, time zones and cultural boundaries. Leading such virtual teams requires very specific organisational knowledge, including how to select qualified experts, knowing which virtual platforms to use and how to structure, support and lead your team. These are among the topics I'll cover in the following pages.

But the coronavirus pandemic has challenged us further. More people than ever before have been working from home in 2020, and we rose to the challenge. This extended period of remote working means we have to take more team decisions remotely, resolve conflicts from a distance and find new ways to lead and manage effectively.

What I want to share with you is that virtual teams can achieve much more. I want to open your eyes to the possibilities available not just to organisations but to society, if we can ignite global talent to address the monumental challenges of our time: Climate change. Hunger. Pandemic response. We have the power to overcome these challenges, all while bringing opportunities to young professionals in every corner of the globe.

PART I

Building Trust and Clarity: Discovering, Dreaming and Goal-Setting

'A dream you dream alone is only a dream. A dream you dream together is reality.'

John Lennon

1

From Failure to Amazing Success in Global Teams

Adam stirs slightly as the dim light of a new day tries its best to break through the fabric of the bedroom curtains. His mind tries to cling to the last strands of his sleep, but he knows that he can't sink back into a deep slumber. Slowly, carefully so as not to wake his wife Rose, he rolls over onto his right side and gropes blindly for the alarm clock.

Through half-closed eyes he sees the blue lines marking out the time: 5:50. At 6:00 a.m. his alarm will start to beep. He sighs, resigning himself to getting out from under the covers. As he stretches and starts to wake his body up, he feels his muscles contracting. They're aching a little after his gym session last night. With a slight groan, he eases himself up to sitting and turns the alarm off. A yawn and a stretch accompanied by some clicks in his body reminds him, once again, that while he's strong for 48 he's not as young as he used to be.

He stands and pads slowly across to the bathroom, flicking on the light and shutting the door behind him. Adam goes through the usual morning rituals. He cleans his teeth, showers, shaves and throws on some aftershave. Wrapped in a towel he makes his way into the bedroom to find Rose is up and has gone downstairs. He dresses for work and gets ready to join his family for breakfast. He can hear the gentle hubbub of his daughter and wife talking in the kitchen.

Adam walks into the kitchen and kisses Rose on the cheek as he passes her to get a cup of coffee. He's barely sat down at the table when Georgia, his daughter, has fixed him with an accusing stare. 'Who bought cheese wrapped in plastic *again*?' she asks, barely giving anyone a chance to answer. 'How many times do I have to say this? There is going to be more plastic than fish in the oceans by 2050, we all have to do our part to change that. Not to mention all the seabirds, dolphins and whales that die each year because they eat plastic. It's disgusting.'

Adam holds his daughter's gaze, trying his best not to erupt and to be reasonable in the face of such an outburst at the breakfast table. 'Look Georgia, I picked up some cheese on my way home from the gym last night. They only had cheese wrapped in plastic. What am I supposed to do? Leave the fridge and cupboard bare for breakfast? Then you'd be complaining you had nothing to eat. One piece of cheese wrapped in plastic isn't going to make a big difference.'

'That's what everyone thinks, and that's why this planet is slowly choking on plastic,' Georgia fires back. 'It's alright for you, but it's my generation who won't have a planet to live on in 50 years. You just exploit the Earth, working in fossil fuels without a care for what it means for the future.' With her eyes burning, Georgia leaves the room before Adam has a chance to respond.

He lets out an audible sigh. Rose reaches across and touches his arm. 'You know how passionate she is about this,' she says in a conciliatory tone. 'Well it wouldn't hurt her to acknowledge how hard I work to put a roof over her head and food on the table,' Adam replies. 'I know, I'll talk to her. She needs to be respectful, even if she doesn't agree with you,' Rose smiles. 'Now, what would you like for breakfast?'

'I think I'll skip breakfast,' Adam says, taking one last sip of his coffee. 'I'll see you later, have a good day.' He gives Rose his best smile as he stands and walks into the hall, but inside he's still angry. He knows his job is far from perfect and he knows that Georgia would much rather he worked in a more, as she puts it, 'responsible' industry. But this is where life has led him. Adam is still thinking about Georgia's remarks when he sits down at his desk half an hour later.

He makes himself a fresh cup of coffee while his computer whirrs into life. The email at the top of his inbox is titled: Confidential. Without entirely knowing why, Adam feels nervous as he opens it. He has to read it through three times before the contents sink in. The gist of it is that they're closing his location because of competition and disruption in the renewable energy sector.

Adam almost laughs in spite of himself. *This should make Georgia happy at least,* he thinks. But then he focuses on the rest of the email. He has two options: take redundancy or relocate to Kuala Lumpur.

The more he reads the email, the angrier he becomes. He's given years of his life to this company, and those are the only two options they can find for him? His breathing has quickened and he realises he's clenching his fists. He slams one down on the desk, spilling a little coffee. *Why the hell have I put so much effort in if this is how I'm going to be treated?*

He takes a deep breath and stands up from his desk, pushing his chair back a little harder than he meant to and feeling a little satisfaction at the sound of the backrest hitting the wall. He walks out of his office to go and see Dave, who's been with the company a little longer than he has. Maybe he'll have better news?

As Adam approaches Dave, he looks up from his computer and gives him a wan smile. 'I take it you got the email too?' Dave says. 'Yep!' Adam replies. 'Where did this come from Dave? It feels like a bolt from the blue. . .' 'Well, I guess the writing's been on the wall for a while if you think about it. We've all known renewables were on the up and disruption is disruption. If you're not going to jump on the bandwagon there aren't many options left.'

Adam can't help but admire how pragmatic Dave is being about all of this. 'Are you moving to KL?' he asks. Dave shakes his head, 'I don't think so. I mean I'll think about it, but I've been thinking about having a change and getting into the renewable energy sector for a few years, so this might just be the push I need, either to go out on my own or to join another company. What are you thinking?'

Adam lets out a sigh. 'Well, I mean, I don't know. I've given 20 years to this company, you know? I'll need to talk to Rose about it. I mean, she's got her coaching business, and then there's Georgia and her schooling. KL could be a good opportunity, but, like you say, maybe this is a nudge to move in a new direction.'

By the time he's walking away from Dave's desk, Adam feels calmer. Dave always does look for the positives in a situation and that was what he needed today, to feel as though there were other options. He hadn't considered moving into renewable energy, despite Georgia's best efforts to convince him in recent months, but now, maybe, just maybe. . .

He doesn't have time for more contemplation though, as he has a video call in, he glances at his watch, in five minutes. He rushes back to his desk, composes himself and gets on with his day. The morning flies by and it's 2pm before he's able to step out for lunch.

As soon as he leaves the office, his thoughts hit him like a speeding train. As he walks his mind flicks between the two scenarios: move to KL with this company, stay in this job and uproot his family, or take the leap of faith into the renewables sector and do something new, something different. His mind keeps returning to Georgia's comments. *This is a chance to do something good for future generations.* But it's terrifying to take that step at this stage in his career. Is he just being idealistic? Adam can't quite tell. *There's a fine line between bravery and stupidity*, he thinks.

Suddenly, he realises how hungry he is and ducks into a nearby takeaway. As he stands waiting to order, he scans the menu. Having skipped breakfast, he's now starving. A burger feels like a good idea, but his eyes drift down the menu and pause on a veggie burger. He knows which Georgia would choose. He's lost in thought and is pulled back to reality by the person behind the counter saying, 'Excuse me, sir, what can I get you?' He smiles, 'I'll have the veggie burger please.'

He collects his burger from the counter and strolls out into the sunshine, making a beeline for the nearest park. Adam finds a bench and settles down, feeling the sun on his face and noticing the breeze in the trees. As he takes a bite of the burger, he starts to realise the possibilities that lie before him. But it's still a big decision to make, and he's not quite ready to take the leap of faith just yet. Maybe he could move to KL? Maybe Rose and Georgia could be happy there?

Walking back to the office, Adam decides he'll apologise to Georgia when he gets home, and then break the news of his impending redundancy, or relocation to KL, to Rose. *That's going to be an interesting conversation.*

Suddenly he remembers Kaito, a Japanese scientist who he met at an energy conference a few years before. They sat next to each other during a seminar about disruption in the solar energy sector and got chatting in the break. Adam can still remember how Kaito's face lit up when he started talking about his work on solar energy projects. It was refreshing to meet someone with so much passion for what he did. *I wonder.* . . Before he has time to think too much about it, Adam gets his phone out of his pocket and fires off a quick message to Kaito. 'Hi Kaito, how's everything going in Japan? I have some exciting news, just wondered if you'd be free for a chat soon?' He knows it's late in Japan, but he's hopeful he'll have a response by morning.

As the rest of the afternoon passes, Adam feels his stomach tying itself in knots. He's not looking forward to the conversation with Rose when he gets home. As he leaves the office, he notices that the wind has picked up and grey storm clouds are looming on the horizon. *Great, what an omen.*

****

As you can see from the beginning of Adam's story, there is a lot to consider when you're creating a virtual team.

I'd like to begin by sharing my definition of a virtual team. This is any team that is in more than one location. This doesn't have to mean that every member of that team is working in a different place. It might be that you have two offices in the same city and team members spread between them. Or you might have some people working from home and others from the office. These people may be working in the same time zones, they may not. For me, a virtual team is any team that communicates virtually at least part of the time.

According to research from Forrester in 2016, 81% of teams are virtual and 60% of these virtual teams are spread across more than one time zone. I'm sure that this figure has increased since this study was carried out. It's also important to understand why you'd want to build a virtual power team.

There are many reasons why this is the most appropriate option. They include expanding your business internationally and delivering projects more quickly, But if you don't spend time creating your virtual power team, there is a good chance they will fail.

I will tell you now that the first time I was a member of a big virtual team, in 2002, my overwhelming emotion was one of frustration. I was one of 30 project managers spread across Europe and our boss was based in London. Once a year we had a face-to-face meeting with everyone in one place. Once a quarter we had a telephone conference, although this was usually an opportunity for our boss to speak and present various KPIs and business results. But aside from these large meetings, we rarely spoke to each other. As a team, we didn't communicate, let alone help one another.

I didn't feel appreciated or recognised by my boss. Over time, I became increasingly frustrated and I'm sure the other project managers did too. This led not only to pain and frustration for us, but also for our manager.

This experience taught me that over time, virtual teams can lose their centre of gravity. People can get lost in space. This leads to a decline in the team's overall performance. It made me question how you could retain this 'gravity' and cohesion over time and even improve a team's performance exponentially as you do so. Before I come onto this though, I'd like to talk to you about why global teams fail.

What Causes Global Teams to Fail?

There are four main reasons why global teams fail. In fact, these are four reasons why any virtual team will fail, not just one that is global.

1. *They fail to build trust* – when you're creating a virtual team you need to make more of an effort to build trust between everyone. They can't bond while using the coffee machine. You need to find ways to build trust despite the distance.
2. *They can't overcome communication barriers* – in virtual teams you have different barriers to overcome. There is the distance and the technology. But there are also potential issues surrounding goal setting, particularly in relation to decision-making and handling conflicts.
3. *The goals of the individual and the team aren't aligned* – sometimes there is a team goal that has been cascaded and not worked out from the bottom up. That means an individual's goal might not align with the team. Or, as is often the case, people within the team have their hidden agendas, whether that's something to facilitate their career or their bonus scheme. If it's not completely aligned with the team's goal, it will lead to issues.
4. *The vision and goal of the team isn't clear* – if the vision and goal has been cascaded, there is a much higher probability of a lack of clarity. By contrast, if people within the team work out the vision and goal together then they identify with it and this is one of the keys to the success of virtual power teams.

What Do All High-Performing Teams Have in Common?

Over the years, I have developed a highly effective method called 'Virtual Power Teams', which comprises 10 Big Rocks. These are the 10 key success factors for retaining the gravity in your team and unleashing the virtual team's power.

I want you to imagine that your virtual team is a human. The first part to consider is the head. This is the logical, cognitive element and it's where you'll find the first three of the 10 Big Rocks that are essential to every virtual power team's success.

These rocks are:

1. Personality in focus
2. The Strengths Matrix
3. Interdependent goals

Personality in focus – this means you need to consider the personalities of every person you include in your team. If, as a manager, you don't believe this is important for remote teams you're making a big mistake. Later on in the book I'll give you an exercise that can help you get to know your team members quickly and intimately. It's important to know how to achieve this when you're managing a remote team. So, the lesson is not to ignore personality when you're choosing your team or recruiting, but instead to put personality in focus.

The Strengths Matrix – this is all about exploring and identifying the key strengths and natural talents of each team member. All too often people can feel anonymous and feel as though they're being treated as a resource. By identifying people's strengths and making everybody else aware of them, you'll make every person in your team feel like a hero who has a special talent that's vital to your success. This is about helping everyone in the team understand that they're not anonymous, but that they're understood. That they've been chosen to be part of this bouquet of skills and with this mix of talent we can achieve anything.

Interdependent goals – goal setting is very important in virtual teams. This rock is about making sure that everyone has their own goal and that everyone is clear on what they need to do to deliver. But more than that, the team will be organised and managed in such a way that they all have the freedom, within budgetary and time constraints, to decide how best to deliver on that goal. Micromanagement is not an option. This is about empowerment. It's about allowing people to set and choose their goals, not simply delegating tasks.

With these three rocks that make up the head of your team, you're aiming for clarity about who your team members are and what goals you're all aiming to achieve.

The next part of the body that I want you to consider is the skeleton and muscles. This is the dynamic part of the body, and therefore of the team. The next three rocks are:

4. Meetings and agenda
5. Knowledge management
6. Regular feedback

Meetings and agenda – this means deciding which online meetings and conferences you need to have as a team. You may have a core leadership team, as well as extended teams, and you need to be clear on how often they will meet and what format these meetings will take.

Knowledge management – this is about how we manage knowledge. It ties in with the Strengths Matrix, but rather than being about skills it's about the knowledge or expertise that individual team members have. I'll talk more later about how you can define knowledge champions or knowledge custodians within your team.

Regular feedback – this can sometimes be scarce in regular teams, but it's even more of an issue in virtual teams. But for your virtual team to be a success, it's essential that you institutionalise feedback. You need to make sure that communication with your team allows everyone to have an equal contribution. You want to establish structured communication where everybody can contribute, rather than taking a manager-centric or problem-centric approach.

From the skeleton and muscles we move onto the heart, which is my personal favourite. There are three rocks that are essential in this part of the 'body':

7. Recognition
8. Diversity
9. Winning spirit

Recognition – did you know that the number one reason for people leaving a company is a lack of recognition by a direct superior. That means people are leaving jobs not because of the company they work for, but because they don't feel recognised by their manager or boss. In virtual teams, it's important to recognise progress despite the distance and I'll give you tips on how you can do this and make sure everyone in your team feels seen.

Diversity – if you have a diverse team from multiple cultures, you need to think carefully about how to establish the optimal team culture. There are three areas in particular that you need to consider: leadership, decision-making and conflict. In leadership, you have the choice between egalitarian and hierarchical and I'll explain how you define the optimal leadership style for your team. With decision-making, you have the choice between top-down and consensus and, again, I'll help you understand how to find the optimal way for your team to make decisions. In terms of conflict, you have confrontational versus non-confrontational approaches. I'll help you reflect and consider different cultural considerations when deciding how best to manage conflict within your team.

Winning spirit – establishing winning spirit in your team when people are spread across time zones and cultures can be challenging. But if you can establish this winning spirit, anything is possible. I'll give you advice on how to establish this winning spirit across your virtual team.

The tenth rock is next generation leaders. This is very important because it is no good having this wonderful virtual power team at the top if there is no one coming through behind them to take their place. You need to make sure you are connected to all the layers of your organisation and think about how you can involve people at all levels in delivering your agenda.

According to Google's Project Aristotle, where they researched the characteristics of high-performing teams, they found that the number one characteristic high-performing teams have is psychological safety.

Google Aristotle

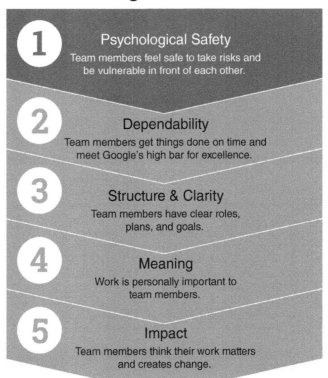

1 Psychological Safety
Team members feel safe to take risks and be vulnerable in front of each other.

2 Dependability
Team members get things done on time and meet Google's high bar for excellence.

3 Structure & Clarity
Team members have clear roles, plans, and goals.

4 Meaning
Work is personally important to team members.

5 Impact
Team members think their work matters and creates change.

This means that the people in those teams are willing to share their vulnerability and don't feel pressure to keep up the appearance of being perfect. The benefit is that when they come up against a task that doesn't play to their strengths, they're not afraid to ask for help. This makes the team a powerful unit. It makes 1+1+1 much more than three.

Establishing Your Foundation

If you lay these 10 Big Rocks, carefully considering each one based on your industry, your locations, the countries your team members are in, their diversity and cultures, your virtual power team will be capable of anything.

Just like when you're establishing the foundations of a big building, you want to make conscious decisions about how you lay your foundation and where you place your 10 Big Rocks. Throughout the rest of this book, I'll share the tools that you

EXPONENTIAL GROWTH

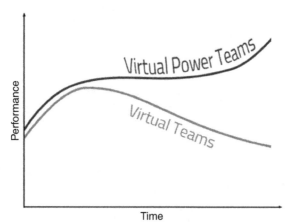

Source: Guide: Understand team effectiveness, re:Work With Google

need to make these conscious decisions to enable your team to become a virtual power team.

I will give you examples of how these rocks have contributed to successful power teams that I've been part of, so that you can see them in action.

2

Personality in Focus

When Adam arrives home, he finds Georgia in the kitchen. 'Georgia, I'm sorry about this morning honey. I know this stuff is really important to you and I will make more of an effort.' 'Thanks Dad,' she says, giving him a hug before leaving to return to her room. He takes off his shoes and jacket and goes in search of Rose, finding her in her home office.

Her face lights up in a beaming smile when he taps lightly on her door, nudging it open to check he's not interrupting. 'How was your day? Better than breakfast I hope?' she asks with a twinkle in her eye. He takes a deep breath and steels himself for what he's about to say. 'Well. . .' 'Adam, what's the matter?' He steps into the room and closes the door, relaying the email, the options and some of his internal monologue to her.

She sits and listens. When he's finished, she looks at him and says, 'You know we can't move to Kuala Lumpur.' He begins to protest, but she silences him with a glance. 'Adam, this isn't just about you. I've got my business here. Georgia is in school. Moving halfway around the world just isn't an option, especially not for a company that treats you like this.' 'I know,' he says with a sigh. *Why do I feel relieved? Did I want her to say no? To be so adamant about staying here?*

'Adam, I know you've put a lot into this job, but maybe it is time to move on? You know I'll support you if you decide you want to go out on your own.' He nods. 'I know, I just wasn't expecting to have such a monumental decision to make this week,' he says, trying to smile. Rose takes his hand, squeezes it and says, 'I know, but you'll do the right thing.'

As Adam sinks into bed that evening, he already knows he's not going to be able to sleep. After his conversation with Rose, he realised that he'd already made his decision. The thought of moving to KL seems laughable now really. Even his choice of lunch had been a sign. He closes his eyes, but all he keeps thinking about is what he needs to do next. It's 11.30 p.m.

He wakes with a start. He can hear the rain lashing against the windows. It's dark but a quick glance at the clock shows him that it's only 1 a.m. Instinctively he reaches for his phone and sees that he has a message from Kaito. His heart's in his mouth. He feels so excited and nervous as he unlocks his phone and opens WhatsApp. 'Hi Adam, great to hear from you. That sounds intriguing. I'm available after work today, I guess that would be about 10.30 a.m. your time?'

Adam can barely contain his grin. He fires a quick message back. 'Kaito, that would be great. I'll speak to you then.'

He lies back down but he can't sleep. His excitement has once again turned to anxiety. *What if I'm making a huge mistake? Can I really do this? What will happen to my family if I get this wrong? What if Georgia's right? What if I could make a positive change with my work? But what if I can't pull this off?*

Adam tosses and turns, falling in and out of sleep, as the rain continues to pour down outside. By 3.30 a.m. he's given up on sleep. He creeps out of the bedroom and downstairs, where he gets his laptop out and starts researching renewable energy innovations to get an idea of where the market is going.

By the time the sun comes up, the rain has been replaced by the sound of birdsong. A bright dart of sunlight has found its way through the break in the curtains and cuts a line across the coffee table. He realises it's 5.55 a.m. He feels suddenly calm though.

He knows what he's going to do and a plan is beginning to form in his mind. He saves his research and closes his laptop, as he softly climbs the stairs and makes his way to the bathroom, Adam allows himself to smile.

When he comes down for breakfast he's feeling much calmer. Rose is chopping fruit and vegetables to make a smoothie, she turns and smiles at him. 'How do you feel today?' she asks. 'You know what, I feel a lot better than I did yesterday,' Adam replies, smiling. 'Could you make me one of those smoothies love?' Rose stares at him for a moment, 'Of course,' she says with a smile. 'What happened to you overnight Dad?' Georgia chips in. 'Don't tell me you've suddenly decided that the planet is worth saving after all?' Adam laughs, 'Actually Georgia, I might be about to make some big changes that will make you very happy!' 'Are you serious? What do you mean?' Georgia looks genuinely excited. 'All in good time. I have a few details I need to hammer out first,' Adam replies.

Georgia keeps bombarding him with questions. 'You can't be that cryptic! What changes are you making? Are you leaving your job? Seriously Dad, tell me, please. . .' 'All I'll say is that I'm exploring my options in the renewable energy space,' he replies. Georgia's eyes light up, 'Really? That's amazing!' she says.

'I have a few calls to make, but I'd love to get your thoughts on it when things are a bit more settled, okay?' he says. 'Yeah, definitely Dad,' Georgia replies. Adam stands and retrieves his smoothie from Rose, who has been listening to the conversation with a smile on her lips.

Then he pauses, glancing briefly at the clock. It's still early. 'Actually, how do you feel about a walk by the lake?' 'Now?' Georgia asks. 'Yeah, I have some time before I need to be in the office and I'd like to run some of my ideas past you.' 'Okay!' Georgia almost bounces out of her chair, popping her breakfast dishes by the sink and racing out of the kitchen to get her coat.

Rose is still watching him. 'Well, you've had quite a turna-round from yesterday!' she says, 'And I'm so happy. Enjoy your walk, just remember Georgia needs to leave for school by 8.30.' Adam grins, 'I know, I'll make sure she's on time, don't worry.'

The path by the lake is peaceful at this time of the morning. Adam is struck by how everything seems to sparkle in the early morning light. While they've been walking, Adam has been telling Georgia about the research he's been doing. They pause, and Georgia says, 'Wind energy is probably the most obvious option. I mean, just look at the offshore wind farms we've got here, not to mention the huge ones up in Scotland.' 'That's a good point,' Adam replies, his mind spinning like a turbine as he starts to consider all the possibilities.

He's forgotten where he is when he feels Georgia's hand on his. 'Dad,' she says, looking at him in a way that she hasn't for quite a long time. 'I'm really proud of you for making this decision.' She leans in and hugs him and in that moment, Adam knows he's making exactly the right choice.

****

The first of these rocks focuses on personality. You might wonder why you should encourage your team members to get to know one another personally; the answer is because it builds trust. When people start connecting with each other as humans, something magical happens.

Instead of firing off a quick email or popping a message on Slack, they pick up the phone or send a personal message. When teams start trusting each other, their performance improves.

If you're starting a business from scratch, like Adam is, chances are that you may well already know at least the first members of your team personally. Remember that they may not all know each other though, so make time to get to know one another in the early days.

How to Start Building Trust in Your Team

There are two exercises you can complete with your team to start building those personal connections.

The first is to get everyone in your team to create a lifeline, a sort of timeline of their lives, that includes their highlights and lowlights. These moments don't have to be professional, they can be personal in nature, too. You can ask people to create just one lifeline, or you can ask them to create two, one for professional moments and one for personal ones.

1. PERSONALITY IN FOCUS

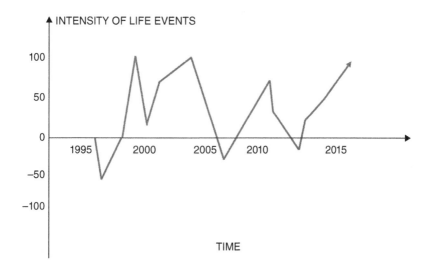

You'll be amazed at how much you can learn about one another in five to ten minutes alone by completing this exercise. I've run this exercise with teams who have been working together for five or even ten years in some cases, and they've learned more about each other during this lifeline exercise than they have in all those previous years of interacting almost daily.

When people explain their lifelines to the rest of the team, you'll learn what makes their heart sing. This sows the seeds for those all-important interpersonal relationships to grow and blossom.

I also tell everyone to bring one photo that they identify with and to share this with the rest of their team. You know the old saying, 'A picture is worth 1,000 words'? It's true.

More and more companies are creating virtual teams who are based all over the world. It allows them to access the best talent out there. But when you're not able to meet face to face, you need to find other ways of building those vital personal relationships and this exercise is a brilliant way to do that.

If you work with a very big team, you can still complete the lifeline exercise. To make sure it doesn't last too long, and that everyone is able to share something about themselves, I have a fast-paced format that you can use instead. Ask everyone to answer the following four questions:

1. Do you have siblings? If so, how many and are they older or younger than you?
2. What hobby were you most passionate about as a child?
3. What are you most proud of?
4. What else should other people know about you?

The aim with these four questions is to provide a small amount of information that people can relate to. The answers people give will spark further conversations, and that's the whole point of this exercise. You can also start to build up a picture of someone based on their answers to these questions.

For example, if they're the oldest sibling in a family they may have taken on a leadership role early in their lives. As the youngest in a family, they may be competitive because they've been trying to keep up with their older siblings. Middle children are often considered to be adaptable, while only children might not be used to sharing.

The first two questions should be easy for anyone to answer and are like a warm-up. The third question is likely to be the one that people need to give the most thought to. And with the fourth question, I'd encourage people to share something exotic, something really unique. These last two questions deliberately encourage people to be vulnerable, to show that less polished side of themselves.

I'll share my answers to these questions so that you can get to know me a little:

1. I have an older brother who lives in Australia (I live in Hamburg, Germany), and he's six years older than me.
2. I used to draw pictures of horses. Usually these were galloping horses being ridden by Native Americans.
3. I'm most proud of my five daughters; they are the apples of my eye.
4. The other thing you should know about me is that I like to throw things over long distances. I was actually the World Champion discus thrower at the competition in Auckland in 2017, and I also took home a bronze medal in the men's over-45 age group javelin competition.

The Importance of Empowerment

During my 20 years in this industry I've led many virtual teams, some of which are spread across different continents and time zones. One of the largest was a European project delivery team that comprised 30 project managers. I have also worked as head of IT for Eastern Europe, the Middle East and Africa, which is not only a huge geographical area but one that can often have poor infrastructure.

Despite all of my experience of managing large global teams, there's one team that I still struggle to manage: my five daughters. However, I have learned lessons about management style from my interactions with them that are transferable to the world of business.

What kind of lessons have I learned from my family that might be applicable in virtual teams? Firstly, when there is a conflict in a virtual team it is often highly charged. Many managers, myself included in the early years, can be guilty of trying to deal with conflict within a virtual team by sending an email. Maybe you send an email and copy a lot of people, which makes the situation worse. Not facing the problem properly creates more problems, but in a virtual team setting it can be easy to hide behind technology. When you send emails like this, you undermine trust and team spirit. I urge you to avoid taking this path.

Start by calling a meeting with the person or people who have contributed to the conflict. Encourage a debate about the situation. Don't set out your opinion upfront, but instead get your team members to share their opinions and suggest solutions. If you do this early and encourage healthy debate, you will save a lot of time and effort further along.

While you're encouraging this debate, strive to find the solution where people choose what they do. You're creating empowerment. When you empower your team in this way, they'll be more committed to the solution you agree on.

If there is one leadership secret I can share with you that I've learned from leading a house of six women, it's not to underestimate the power of praise. So praise, praise and then praise some more.

Praise the result, if there's a result. Praise a sub-milestone that someone achieves. Even if they haven't achieved anything, praise positive behaviour. If you can't see anything immediately that you can praise, look harder. There will be something there and this encouragement is the way to start improving performance, even from a distance.

The following are some questions for you to consider at this stage. They're self-coaching questions and I invite you to write down your answers before continuing with the rest of this book.

1. Do you know your virtual team's personal interests, passions and strengths?
2. How can the unique personality of each team member find expression in the team?
3. How do you sustain interpersonal relationships over time and build on them for team success?

3

The Strengths Matrix

In the office, time seems to stand still as Adam waits for his 10.30 a.m. call with Kaito. Eventually, it's time to connect. He dials into the Zoom meeting and waits for Kaito to join him. 'Adam, hi! It's so good to see you. How are you?' Adam breaks into a broad grin. 'I'm great thanks. It's great to see you too. Look, Kaito, things have changed for me recently and I've decided I want to make a go of it in the renewable energy space.' He pauses, waiting for a reaction. Kaito smiles, then laughs. 'That's fantastic! What are you thinking about?' 'Well, for a start I'd really love you to be involved. . .'

The half hour whizzes past as Adam and Kaito talk back and forth about all the options in the sector. A plan is beginning to fall into place, although Adam is in favour of wind energy following his talk with Georgia and given what he's seen happening off the Norfolk coast, while Kaito prefers the idea of solar. Both of them are very passionate about their preferred options, and neither is prepared to back down.

After half an hour of going round in what feels like circles, with Adam and Kaito reiterating their respective preferences for wind or solar, Adam is getting tired and frustrated. He knows he needs to put a stop to the conversation.

He interjects, 'Kaito, look, I hear what you're saying but I really think that wind is the direction we should go in. I'll do some research on the solar projects you're talking about, but I want to start with wind energy and build from there.'

Kaito's expression changes ever so slightly. Adam thinks he looks slightly crestfallen. What Adam can't see is that Kaito, who has been making notes on a pad next to his laptop, is scribbling hard on the pad, scoring deep, dark lines into the crisp white paper.

'Right, well, I guess I'll wait to hear from you then,' Kaito says abruptly.

Adam seems unaware of the note of frustration running through Kaito's voice. 'Great,' he says, 'I'll be in touch later this week.'

They say their goodbyes and log off. Adam sits back and exhales. He hadn't been aware that he was holding his breath. *I'm doing the right thing. I know more about the wind sector than solar. Kaito will come around.* He continues with his day but there's a niggling sense of unease settling into his thoughts.

****

When Adam returns home that evening, he's still mulling over his call with Kaito. He's been thinking about it on and off all day. As he enters the house, he can hear Rose in the kitchen. He slips off his shoes, loosens his tie and walks down the hall. As he enters the kitchen, he's visibly preoccupied.

Rose is dipping a herbal tea bag in a mug of hot water. As she swirls it around trails of deep purple stain the water. Adam looks at what she's making and pulls a face. 'You don't fancy one of these then?' Rose asks with a smile and a twinkle in her eye. 'I honestly don't know how you can drink that stuff,' Adam replies. He gets himself a glass of water and sits down at the table, pulling his phone out of his pocket as he does so and allowing it to drop onto the table in front of him.

'How was your day?' Rose asks, 'Did you speak to your Japanese colleague?' Adam looks up at her and pauses. 'I did,' he says. Rose eyes him somewhat suspiciously. 'Do I take it from your tone that the meeting didn't go well?'

'Well, it wasn't exactly what I'd expected,' Adam admits. 'I thought he'd be really excited to get onboard but he kept talking about solar projects and I really want to focus on wind energy, at least initially. It felt like we were going round in circles so I just put my foot down and told him wind was the way to go.'

He pauses. Rose picks up her tea having removed the tea bag and sits next to Adam at the table. 'Do you think it was wise to just dismiss his views? I thought you said he was an expert,' she asks.

'He is, but I mean, it's my company and I have an idea of where I want it to go,' Adam says, almost with a touch of petulance in his tone.

'I understand that you're excited about this and, believe me, I am too, and so is Georgia. But Adam, you've worked in oil for the last 20 years. I know that you've had some involvement with wind energy because of what happens locally, but I thought the whole point of this meeting was to get the input of an expert in this space, the renewable energy space?'

Rose waits for a response. Adam's gaze shifts and he looks at his phone. The message light is blinking. 'Adam, come on, I'm just trying to help. I want you to make this work and I know that's what you want too.'

He looks up at Rose and can see that she's concerned. 'Well what would you have done?' he asks.

'Did you listen to his reasons for wanting to focus on solar energy? Were they valid?' she asks.

'I told him I'd do some research and that I'd consider it,' Adam replies.

'That's not what I asked. . .' Rose shakes her head slightly. Adam looks away again. The message light on his phone is still blinking. 'Adam, you are going to have to approach this slightly differently to your job at the moment. I know you're used to being able to dictate exactly what happens, but you need to be a bit more collaborative with this venture.'

'You think I should speak to Kaito again and consider switching to solar instead of wind?' he asks, with a hint of disbelief in his voice.

'I'm not saying you have to change your opinion, but you should definitely be open to that idea,' she says. 'He's an expert in his field and there's a reason why you chose to contact him. That's all I'm saying.'

'But I said I'd research it and go back to him. I didn't completely dismiss his ideas. . .' Adam's voice trails off.

Rose is still looking at him, even though he can't meet her gaze. 'That's not quite the same thing as listening to him though, is it?' she asks, not really expecting a response.

Adam sighs, 'No, I suppose not, but what am I supposed to do? Just do whatever anyone else wants? That's no way to run a business.' He's starting to raise his voice.

'That's not what I'm saying either,' Rose says, in a calm and even tone. 'You know that's not what I'm saying. Just answer me this, why do you want Kaito to be involved?'

'Because he knows so much about the renewable space and he's been working in that sector for years,' Adam answers instantly, adding, 'And because I trust him, we have a good relationship.'

Rose smiles. 'There you go then, you know what you need to do.' She reaches out and squeezes his arm. Adam looks at her. 'You're doing the right thing and you'll do great things, just remember that you can't do this alone and we all have our strengths.' She leans in and hugs him. Adam lets out a sigh as his arms tighten around his wife. 'What would I do without you?' he asks.

****

When Adam checks his messages after dinner, he sees that one is from Kaito asking to talk. After his talk with Rose he's feeling much calmer and has realised that he needs Kaito's input. He suggests another call the following day at the same time. To his immense relief, Kaito agrees.

Adam is restless when he goes to bed. He tosses and turns and is constantly woken by the sound of the wind racing through the trees outdoors. The more he focuses on the need to sleep, the harder he finds it to disconnect. He's relieved when he sees the first shafts of sunlight breaking through the gap in the curtains.

Although he's the first out of bed, he's the last one to reach the kitchen for breakfast in the morning. Georgia greets him with a smile and Rose offers him coffee. 'What do you want for breakfast?'

'I'm not really hungry,' Adam replies, sounding slightly distracted. 'I've got another call with Kaito this morning,' he adds by way of explanation. Rose smiles, 'That's great,' she says. 'I hope so,' Adam replies.

'Who's Kaito?' Georgia pipes up. 'He's a guy that I'm hoping to work with on this new venture,' Adam explains. 'Cool! Is he an expert in wind energy?' she asks, beaming. 'Actually, he's a solar expert,' Adam responds. 'You're going to do solar too? That's awesome, there's so much potential for solar energy, especially in places like Africa,' Georgia says. 'Well, that's what we're going to talk about today,' Adam adds. He doesn't want Georgia to get too excited about this just yet.

'I'd better get going,' he says, glancing at his watch. He downs the last of his coffee, planting a kiss on Rose's lips as he passes her to put his mug in the sink. He kisses the top of Georgia's head as he leaves the kitchen and for once she doesn't protest. In spite of feeling concerned, Adam is smiling by the time he gets in his car.

****

Adam has butterflies in his stomach as 10.30 a.m. approaches at work. When he dials into the call with Kaito he's nervous and relieved when Kaito greets him warmly. After his talk with Rose last night he'd been worried that he'd really upset his friend.

'I just have something I'd like to say,' Kaito begins. Adam's heart sinks. *He's going to say he doesn't want to come in on the venture.* 'I felt as though you didn't really listen to me properly yesterday and I think that's a mistake. There is so much potential in solar energy and I'm well positioned to help you take advantage of that. I'm not dismissing wind energy out of hand, but I really think that solar is the place to start to build a strong foundation. . .'

Adam cuts in, 'Kaito, I'm sorry that I seemed so dismissive yesterday. And you're right, I didn't really listen properly. Please can you talk me through your points again? I want to take notes so I can do some research myself.'

Kaito visibly brightens. He seems to sit up straighter and there's a new energy to his speech. 'Sure, I'm really pleased you want to work through this thoroughly.'

After half an hour, Adam can see why Kaito was so keen to start with solar energy and he is beginning to appreciate the business case for doing so. But his heart is still set on wind energy. *Maybe we could do both?*

'This has been great, thank you,' Adam says warmly and he means it. 'I still want to go away and do a bit of research myself before we settle on solar along with wind, particularly in relation to the market in the UK, but I can feel myself leaning in your direction now.'

Kaito breaks into a grin. 'Of course, I wouldn't expect you to make a decision like this immediately. I've got some notes that I'll send via email, it's just a few places where you can look for research and so on. It'll save you a bit of time anyway.'

'Great, I'll pull together my research on wind energy and send that over to you as well. Where do we go from here?' Adam asks.

'We'll definitely need a financial expert,' Kaito says, 'Someone who can help us to raise the funds we need. How about Jeff? The guy from California who we met at that conference in 2012? Are you still in touch with him?' Adam nods. 'I am actually. I'll get in touch with him as soon as we're off this call and set up a meeting for the three of us.'

****

The second rock for building your virtual power team is what's known as the Strengths Matrix. I'm a big believer in strength-oriented management, which means you strengthen the strength instead of developing the weakness.

This isn't a new concept and it's certainly not my invention. In fact, Gallup has a book called *StrengthsFinder 2.0*, which includes a very sophisticated test with 64+ questions to establish your key strengths and develop an action plan.

For virtual teams, I believe we need a more pragmatic approach that delivers faster solutions. There's an exercise I use, after the lifeline exercise I discussed earlier in this section, where I ask people to list their top strengths. I'll share the exercise with you in more detail in a moment, but first you need to understand why it's so important to identify each team member's strengths.

The reason is remarkably simple: if you discover someone's true strength, their real natural talent, and focus their work on this area then they don't consider it to be work. They feel joy, they're passionate and often the results are outstanding.

In general, I would say that there are three types of people:

- Generalists
- Specialists
- Empaths

Generalists have a broad overview of what's going on and understand the big picture. These are the kinds of people that you want to put in roles where they're responsible for managing a particular client or stakeholder group. They'll maintain a relationship with those people and channel and manage any demands through the team.

Specialists have deep expertise in a particular field. These are the kinds of people I would nominate as knowledge champions in their field. That means that every time there's a deliverable within the team that falls under their area of expertise, they review it and suggest improvements or give feedback before it's disseminated more widely. In doing this, you show them that their expertise is valued.

Finally, there are empaths. These are the kinds of people who have a good sense of the emotion within the team and who are naturally great at relating to other people and fostering a positive team atmosphere. You might give them responsibility for taking care of a new team member induction, for instance. Even if your HR team has an induction process, don't underestimate the benefits of giving them a buddy, so to speak, within the team they're joining. These people are key.

Those are some basic examples of how you can leverage someone's natural strengths to generate additional meaningful interactions and improve team spirit.

Think back to Adam's story. What groups would you put his early team members into? It's fair to say that Kaito is a specialist. Adam is a generalist. Would you also class Jeff as a specialist? At this stage, Adam's wife Rose is playing the part of the empath.

How to Uncover People's Natural Strengths

I like to believe that everyone has a superpower. It's what I call people's natural strengths.

Uncovering each person's superpower is essential for building an effective virtual team. I'm going to give you a simple exercise now that you can try with your team. Begin by splitting into pairs. One person will be the coach and the other will answer the questions, then they'll swap. Here the questions everyone should ask (and answer):

1. What do you find easy and fun to do in your job?
2. What is your biggest success so far?

3. What do people most often ask you for help with?
4. If I were to ask your best friend what your biggest strength is, what would they say?
5. From everything you've just told me, what do you think your biggest strength is?

Then the coach says, 'From everything I just heard, I think your biggest strength is....'

By the end of this exchange, you should have two strengths listed for each person. One that they have identified themselves and one that their 'coach' has identified. Capture both of these strengths in the Strengths Matrix. I'd encourage you to use different colours for each, for example red for the individual perspective and blue for the external perspective.

The next step in this exercise is for each person to share their superpowers with the rest of the team. But before they do that, give them some time to come up with an avatar who shares their strengths. This can be a comic book character, a superhero, a celebrity, a politician – anyone who inspires you. This brings some humour and fun to the exercise.

What you find when you go through this exercise, especially after having plotted everyone's lifelines as I discussed in the last chapter, is that everyone begins to feel special because they can see the strengths and talents they're bringing to the table. But this also has an incredible effect on the team as a whole, who will now feel as though they can achieve anything they set their minds to because of the Strengths Matrix they can see before them.

The other advantage to setting up a Strengths Matrix is that you'll improve everyone's enjoyment of their job and therefore their quality of work. By allowing people to work on tasks that play to their strengths, not only will they enjoy their job more but they'll be more productive and produce better outcomes as a result.

This will also be important when it comes to setting goals and building a roadmap for your team. Once you have created a Strengths Matrix, you won't need to delegate tasks. Your team members can choose their own goals and tasks based on their strengths. This leverages their talent and creates more 'gravity' within your team. Remember how important that is for bringing everyone together and keeping them focused.

How this Works in Practice

I'd like to give you a real-life example of where this worked in practice. I have a client in New York, who runs a massive open online course (MOOC) teaching modern architecture. To prevent this from being too dry, he has a live case study that everyone on the course works on.

The case study is designing and building resilient schools in the Philippines. You may remember that this country has suffered from earthquakes and tsunamis in the past. As a result of these natural disasters, the government in the Philippines decided to construct schools that were robust enough to enable them to be used as emergency shelters in the event of natural disasters such as these.

This was a six-week course during which time my client provided guidance through videos. Participants didn't pay for the course until they had successfully completed it and received their certification.

He had over 35,000 people sign up for the course. He also had a team of 20 professors who were providing feedback on the designs that the students were creating.

The aim was to have a completed school design by the end of the sixth week. But as soon as it reached the fifth week, he saw a significant drop in the number of students. Many people were learning for five weeks, but when it came to completing the course and paying for their certificate, they just weren't interested.

As a result he changed his approach and asked for the fees up-front. But this meant only 2,000 people signed up to his MOOC. By the time we had an online coaching workshop together, he was in trouble.

We decided that he should go back to the approach of taking payment on completion of the course, but that he'd focus on significantly increasing conversions to the final week and therefore payment. How did we do this?

To begin with, we decided to split this massive group of 35,000 people into groups of five. It sounds like a mammoth task, but we got the students to self-organise and choose their groups based on factors like proximity, time zone and so on.

Once people had split into a group of five, they were invited to an online session where they each presented their lifeline and then discovered their strengths using the five questions I outlined above. Based on what they found out through these exercises, they then split the work from the project between the five of them.

Once the critical week, week five, arrived, they were invested in their team and they couldn't let their teammates down. This led to his conversions increasing to 20,000 completions of the course and payments.

For my client, this resulted in a $480,000 boost to his revenues, all just by using these two simple techniques I've just talked you through.

Why Personality in Focus and the Strengths Matrix is a Magic Combination

The reason why these two techniques can have such a powerful effect on the success of virtual, and indeed any, teams is that they give every team a vision. In the corporate world there is often a corporate vision that is cascaded down to teams. The problem with cascading a vision down, is that there will often be elements of the corporate vision that some people find it hard to identify with.

My approach works the opposite way. As a team leader you can choose one of these two options. The first is the Martin Luther King 'I have a dream' approach, where you explain the team vision in such a vivid way that everyone follows you. The second is to let everyone in your team work out the vision.

I always recommend that virtual teams choose the second option, even if you are Martin Luther King. Why? Because people will identify with every part of the vision if it's something they contribute to themselves.

How to Create a Team Vision

This may not be the precise definition of a vision, but it will help your team to focus and allow them all to use their superpowers to best effect.

Begin by breaking your team into five groups (depending on how many people you have) and ask the first group to consider the purpose of your team. They need to ask the question, 'Why do we do what we do?'

Start with Why by Simon Sinek is an excellent book that explores this concept and looks at what makes 'Why?' such a powerful question. Understanding your 'Why' as a team will give you a lot of energy to tackle your first problem together.

Ask the second group to explore who your target audience is. Who are you trying to reach? What channels are you selling your products through? How do you look after your customers?

The third group should work on identifying the unique selling proposition or unique value proposition. They should answer the question of 'What's unique about our team?' and from there identify your value proposition.

The fourth group should consider what your customers get from you that they can't get from anywhere else.

And the fifth group should identify the key resources within the team, and also explain what your team members can get within the team that they can't get anywhere else.

Firstly, allow everyone to contribute individually to the question assigned to their group. In doing so, you give the more introverted team members a chance to contribute effectively and allow everyone to recognise their own word or contribution in the vision statement.

Give each group some time to work on their question together as well and then pass their suggestions on to the next group and so on, until every group, and every person, has considered all five questions. If you're all in the same location you might use five different flipcharts to collect everyone's ideas, but if you're doing this virtually you can use virtual whiteboards. The contributions don't need to be big. They just need to be a few key words or a short sentence for each area.

The key is to ensure that every individual within each of those groups has an opportunity to contribute. You need to make sure that the introverts are encouraged to speak up and aren't spoken over by the extroverts.

Once every group has provided their thoughts on all five of these questions, ask each group to formulate a sentence using all the key words that feature across the whiteboards. This sentence needs to be neither too short nor too long, but it needs to encompass the team's purpose and its essence. Encourage everyone to discuss their ideas as a big group once the smaller groups have finished their discussions.

When you combine what all five groups have come up with, you'll have a team vision. It might need some fine tuning, but the most important thing is that everyone will know they've made a contribution and everyone in your team will identify with the vision.

Once you've reached this stage, you can begin breaking that vision into strategic goals, which is what I'll talk about in the next chapter.

4

Interdependent Goals

As Kaito closes the meeting he sits back in his chair and lets out a sigh, although instead of scribbling angrily on his pad this time he's grinning. He knew Adam would come around to renewable energy being the future. He'd known that as soon as they got talking at the conference a few years ago, and he's pleased his friend has finally decided to take the plunge – and with solar hopefully! *This is good for me. There's so much in development with solar at the moment, we have a real chance to disrupt the sector in a good way.* Kaito suddenly snaps out of his thoughts, staring at the twinkling lights of Tokyo out of his window. *Imagine if they were all powered by solar energy?* He turns back to the room, glancing at the small clock on his desk. It's 19:40, he'll need to hurry if he's going to make his Aikido class at the Dojo.

****

Back in Norfolk, Adam is sitting at his desk and he's buzzing. It's very different to how he felt the day before. As he gets up to go to the kitchen, he spots Dave across the office. *I wonder, maybe I should see if Dave wants to get onboard with this? His supply chain expertise could be really useful.* Adam waves and makes his way over to where Dave is sitting. 'Dave, do you have time to go for a walk later? There's something I wanted to chat to you about,' Adam says. 'Sure, say one-ish?' 'Great,' Adam smiles and heads for the kitchen.

When he returns to his desk, he writes two emails. One to his bosses, telling them that he'll be leaving the company and won't be moving to KL, and the other to Jeff in California, outlining his new venture and asking if he'd be interested in getting involved.

****

Jeff always wakes early. He's the kind of person who bounces out of bed as soon as his alarm goes off. He stretches, pulls on his running gear and leaves the house for his usual run. The city is just waking up at this time of day. The streets are empty save for the garbage collectors and the odd jogger. He feels good as his feet pound the tarmac.

When he returns home a little over an hour later, he can hear the kids stirring in their rooms. Emily is singing to herself, or perhaps her dolls, he's never quite sure, and he can hear Ben rooting through his toy box as Jeff makes his way to the bathroom for a shower. Lisa emerges from their bedroom as he's stepping into the bathroom. 'Good run?' she asks. 'Always,' Jeff replies with a big grin, planting a kiss on her lips before closing the bathroom door.

Jeff never checks his phone or emails until after breakfast. These first hours of the day are for exercise and family, nothing more. When he sits down to read his emails he's not surprised to see one from Adam. He'd heard on the grapevine that the company Adam worked for was planning to cut back its UK operations. Something to do with the British government's renewable energy sector deal and the push for a more environmentally friendly energy mix. Still, he's intrigued to find out how this has affected Adam. He opens the email and starts reading. *Huh, well there's an idea I can get onboard with. Great to see that he's got Kaito involved, he's been leading on some really exciting research recently. His expertise in the solar sector will be invaluable*. He replies, telling Adam he'll have time for a meeting on Monday.

****

Just as Adam is getting ready to leave the office and head home for the day, he sees a reply from Jeff ping into his inbox. He opens it and feels the excitement building as he reads Jeff's response. His team is falling into place. He's so excited he can barely wait for the meeting, but he's keen to get something in the diary straightaway. Hurriedly, he sends out a meeting invite for the following Monday to Jeff and Kaito. He sets it for 6 p.m. UK-time, without thinking about the time difference.

The next morning, he wakes to a message from Kaito. 'About that meeting on Monday – did you mean to organise it for 2 a.m. Tokyo time?' Adam feels a flush of embarrassment. He hadn't even thought about the time difference, he'd been too excited. Before replying, he sits down to work out when he can rearrange the meeting for. With California eight hours behind the UK and Tokyo eight hours ahead, someone is going to have to compromise and get up in the middle of the night and he realises it will need to be him. He apologises to Kaito and resends the meeting invite for 1 a.m. UK-time on the Tuesday morning. That will make it 5 p.m. in California on Monday, and 9 a.m. in Tokyo on Tuesday.

****

Adam can barely wait for Monday to be over. He takes a nap in the evening and gets up in plenty of time for the meeting. After the usual pleasantries and a brief catch-up, they start to get down to business. Jeff's first question catches Adam off guard. 'Adam, in your email you mention wind and solar energy, but I think solar is the better of the two options, there's just more potential. From a financing perspective that's blowing up over here. You'll have a lot more options for venture capital if you go down the solar route. Plus, Kaito has experience in this area too.' 'I hear you,' Adam says. 'But I'd really like to keep wind energy on the table.

It's such an important part of the energy mix in the UK,' 'You have to think bigger than the UK,' Jeff chips in. 'There are some fantastic global opportunities in this sector and I really think that solar is the sector with the greatest growth potential. Kaito, what do you think?'

'There's definitely potential in both areas,' Kaito says. 'Based on the conversations I'm having here, solar is looking like it could be bigger, but then this is just one market and there is definitely interest in wind energy too.' Adam feels a little deflated. 'After our last conversation I got the feeling you were leaning towards wind energy too?' Adam asks Kaito. 'I think it's an area we still need to discuss and research further,' Kaito says. The three of them continue to talk for a further 20 minutes, at which point Adam realises they're no closer to a resolution.

'Look guys, I think we have to leave it here for today. We're just going round in circles and we're not any closer to agreeing,' Adam says eventually. Kaito steps in, 'Why don't we each do some research in our area of expertise, then we can discuss it and decide what makes the most sense going forward?' Adam and Jeff nod. Kaito continues, 'Jeff can look into the financial aspects of wind and solar. I'll do some more digging on the science, and Adam, can you look at business models?' They agree to catch up again the following week and Adam logs off. He sits at his computer for a while, just staring at the screen, before making his way to bed. It's 2.30 a.m.

****

The next morning he wakes feeling frustrated. He's quiet at the breakfast table and Rose can tell something's wrong. When Georgia goes to get ready for school, she asks Adam what's wrong. He talks her through the meeting of the previous night. 'I just thought we'd agreed on wind with solar as an add on, and it feels as though we're stuck in a rut,' he sighs.

'I think you need to take a different approach to this,' Rose says. 'Think about how great it is that you all have such passion for different areas. But really this shouldn't be about which option you prefer, it should be about which one makes the most business sense and which one can make the greatest positive difference.' Adam knows she's right. 'Kaito's idea is a good one. You all need to play to your strengths when you're starting a new business. It's different to the corporate world,' she adds.

It is different, Adam realises. *This is going to be a steeper learning curve than I thought!* 'Thanks love, you're right. It's still early days and we're working out how to be a team and how to work together.' He feels his frustration ease. He knows what he has to do and he's ready to take on the challenge.

****

I'd like to start this chapter by asking you a question: Have you ever worked on a project where you give everything, but there are other members of your team who aren't so motivated? When I ask this question in workshops, almost everyone will say, 'Yes'.

In virtual teams, it can be even more likely that this scenario will happen, because people can deliberately postpone their responses by not answering their mobile phone, or choosing not to reply to emails for a day or two.

This is what I call 'hiding behind a virtual corner' and I would say that it's a scenario that is much more likely in virtual teams.

To tackle this and prevent this scenario from happening, I would break down the vision and annual strategic goal into as many goals as necessary that everyone on the leadership team has his or her own goal. When I say leadership team, I'm referring to big teams in a corporate environment where you would have a senior manager with their own teams under them and direct reports who form the extended leadership team. What we're aiming for is to build a virtual power team within this structure.

Do you know the optimum size of a team? They call it a 'two pizza team', which means that if you work late and order pizza two will be sufficient. That means the optimum size for a team is seven, plus or minus two. That means you need between five and nine people for your virtual power team.

Once you have your team members, you're aiming to ensure that every person is happy with his or her strategic goal.

Start by Defining the Hottest Issues for your Team

You need to begin this process by defining the top three hottest issues or opportunities for your team.

Even if you're the smartest manager, if your team is spread across multiple locations or even multiple countries, you simply are not in a position to define these three hottest issues. You have to do this bottom-up.

Silhouette Exercise

There's a simple way to approach this though. Firstly, break the team into three groups. Do this randomly, so that you don't just end up with people who usually work together in the same groups. Don't forget to include yourself in one of these groups too.

In the first group, start by drawing the silhouette of a human with wings and a heart. Get each person to complete the following exercise individually initially. Once you have the silhouette, ask the following questions:

1. What turns your head?
2. What lies in your heart?
3. What are your hands itching for?
4. What does your gut feel say?

5. What baggage or chains weigh down your feet?
6. What can give you wings?
7. What can untie your hands?

After each question, capture the key words or short sentences next to the relevant body part of your silhouette.

I've deliberately selected provocative questions which will tease out some of the issues, opportunities, goals and even fantasies related to the team.

You can work through this exercise in these small groups, but encourage each person to capture their own individual thoughts and perspective for each of the seven questions.

The second group, meanwhile, is working on the issues and opportunities. Split a whiteboard into two sections, labelling them 'Issues' and 'Opportunities'. This group will be working as a team to write down everything they can think of that comes under one of these two categories in relation to the team. Remind them that they don't need to come up with solutions to issues, they simply need to capture them. If there are any disagreements, capture them all at this stage.

Finally, the third group gets a creative assignment. They need to draw the symbol of success for the team. The point is to make this inspirational for the team themselves, they have to come up with it.

Once all three groups have finished their assignments, you bring the team back together and each group presents their results. The key to identifying the three hottest issues and opportunities isn't to let the boss decide, but for everybody to vote.

Each person is given three votes and they have to allocate these to what they feel are the three most important issues or opportunities across the silhouette, the issues/opportunities board and the symbol of success.

Once everyone has placed their votes, you count up to see which topics have got the most attention. They could all be issues, they could all be opportunities, they could all be goals, or they could be a mix.

If you have similar topics you might categorise them in a meaningful way and if you end up with multiple topics with the same number of votes you can have a discussion within the team about them.

At the end of this exercise, you will have identified the three hottest topics for your team.

This is a very revealing and relieving exercise. It's an opportunity for everyone in the team to have a voice. This is especially important for virtual teams, because often they will just be delegated assignments, they might get praise but they might not. This is an opportunity to capture their emotions and thoughts. As a result, they will feel more motivated because they have helped to shape the agenda.

The Thinking Behind SMART Goals

Once you have identified your three hottest issues, you need to turn these into SMART goals.

But before we go into creating SMART goals, I'd like to explain the thinking behind them.

You start with 'Why?'. If you know why you do what you do, you'll have much more energy to overcome problems.

Then you move onto 'Who?'. Before you define the goal, you need to know who will be assessing whether it's a success or a failure. You need to identify the key stakeholders, which should include the members of the team, as well as any other stakeholders, and how they would measure whether you've been successful.

Next you look at 'What?'. This is the SMART goal itself.

Finally, you go to 'How?', which is how you can achieve this goal. Once you've answered all of these questions, you can come up with a roadmap or a high-level timeline.

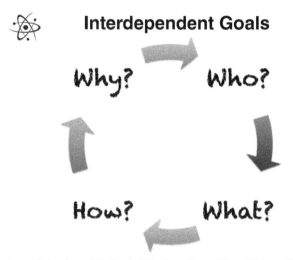

Interdependent Goals

Special thanks to Kimberly Wiefling from Silicon Valley alliances (SVA) for the graph (Why-Who-What-How) and systematic approach related to the SMART goals setting.

There are a number of tools you can use to make sure you not only identify the right SMART goals, but also that everyone on the team is motivated to achieve them.

With 'Why?', it's important to ask this question five times. Once you answer 'Why?' the first time, you need to look at the answer and ask, 'But why this?'. Do this at least twice, but ideally five times to go deep enough to find the real 'Why?'. When you do this, one of two things will happen. Either you'll discard the goal, because you realise the why isn't strong enough, or you'll have much more commitment to achieving it because you understand the real why.

Under 'Who?' use stakeholder and communication maps and analysis to identify everyone involved. Under 'What?' define the SMART goal and your priorities.

Next, ask the very important question, 'Why not?'. This is where you explore the risks and obstacles to make sure that everyone is clear upfront about any potential issues you might face.

Once you get to the 'How?' you're ready to create your roadmap and high-level plans for achieving that goal.

Creating SMART Goals

Return to your three hottest topics and turn these into SMART goals. The first thing you need to do is turn any negative statements into positives – that means you state what it is that you want, rather than what you don't want. Then you cover each of the five elements that makes a goal SMART.

SMART stands for:

- Specific – define why we do it (remember to ask this question five times), what the key characteristics are, what will be different, who the key stakeholder is and what that stakeholder will say if you are wildly successful. You're using these questions to make the goal more personal and tangible to everyone in the team.
- Measurable – define what the key metric is. How will you know you've achieved the goal? How will the key stakeholder(s) measure your success?
- Agreed – think about who can help you, who can hurt you and who else is impacted. Whose approval do you need?
- Realistic – consider what resources you need. This will include your budget.
- Time bound – when will you achieve this goal by? It's very important to have a specific deadline.

If you use all of these techniques to define and formulate your SMART goals, you'll be amazed by the level of engagement you get and the amount of energy your team will put into achieving these goals.

But remember, this concept of creating interdependent goals is just one of the 10 Big Rocks that you need to unleash your team's full potential.

Name your Team

Once you have defined your SMART goals, ask the team to come up with a team name. This name should be emotionally related to the stakeholders, or the success that the team foresees. It should be a funny, emotionally strong team name. You should also come up with a team gesture, which will usually be related to the name.

Why a gesture as well as a name? This is something that you can do online in front of a camera and it's a way of getting everyone on the team to bond.

Developing your Roadmap

This is the 'how'. Begin by writing today's date on one side of the whiteboard, and the deadline that is listed in the SMART goal on the other side. Create one of these for each of the three SMART goals you've identified and split your team back into their three groups.

Give everyone in your team sticky notes (or access to the virtual whiteboard if you're not all in the same place) and get everyone involved in building the roadmap. Each group will tackle one of the goals.

Ask the question: To achieve this goal, what are the key deliverables and the key milestones?

You'll be amazed at how easily and quickly people are able to come up with these milestones if you have a proper SMART goal and if the members of your team are emotionally attached to it.

Before they finalise their roadmaps though, ask each group to imagine that they have already achieved the goal. Then get them to ask themselves two questions:

1. What have we missed?

2. What advice can we give ourselves now that will allow us to achieve this goal even faster and better?

Normally, you will see one or two sub-goals or milestones added to the roadmap, or you might notice that they'll refine the timing even further. Once the roadmaps are completed, you get each group to present the roadmap for their SMART goal.

Sharing Responsibility

Once each roadmap has been presented, ask everyone in the team to choose several milestones that will be their responsibility. It's very important that people voluntarily take ownership of each particular deliverable and that you, as the manager, don't just delegate the tasks.

Each person will justify their choices using their strengths that were identified in the Strengths Matrix exercise. By doing this, everyone on your team will feel much more empowered and motivated to achieve these goals. Micromanagement isn't an option with virtual teams and, in fact, will hold you back.

As a team, they have come up with the goals, they have defined them and refined them. They've set their own strategic agenda. They have explained exactly how they plan to achieve these goals and, in doing all of this, you've empowered them to achieve those goals.

Getting the Best from your Team

In every team, you have the top 10% who are the highest performers. They are ambitious and they will give their all to put in a strong performance. Then you have 75% who are what I call the 'good citizens'. They might not be as ambitious, but without them you can't deliver the project and hit your targets. Then you have the bottom 10–15% who are the lower performers, not necessarily people you need to fire, but they're the ones who would usually hide behind the virtual corners.

By making sure that everyone in the team is responsible for their own strategic goal(s), you eliminate those virtual corners. You'll also see some healthy peer pressure, with the high performers and good citizens putting pressure on the low performers to up their game and thereby improve the overall performance of the team.

The final point here is that these goals are interdependent. That means they lead to meaningful interactions within the team. Each person has to interact with other team members to deliver their strategic goal. Everyone has to support each other and cooperate with one another.

This is another way of fostering the all-important gravity in your team and helping to improve your team's overall performance.

PART II

Establishing Structured Communication: Active Collaboration and Coopetition

5

How Everyone Can
Contribute and Shine

Adam is sitting at his laptop, furiously tapping away at the keyboard. He's getting a few glances from the other customers in Starbucks who can see he's getting frustrated but he doesn't care. He takes another sip of his coffee. 'Bing'. He ignores the cue from the bottom of his screen telling him that he has another email. 'Bing' And then another. He tries to focus on what he's writing. He's nearly finished this. . . 'Bing' 'Bing' 'Bing'. His inbox is filling up.

Slightly exasperated, he opens his inbox to see 76 unread messages, 15 of which have arrived in the last five minutes. He sighs and starts opening them, firing off replies, forwarding any that he thinks Jeff, Kaito, Dave or their solar expert Sunita needs to see.

There's a chain of emails at the top of his inbox that keeps growing. He opens this one and sees that it was initiated by Sunita. *Not today. I have so much to do right now.* It's about the R&D for their new solar project. She wants a call that afternoon at 4 p.m. his time. Adam groans. That would mean going back to the co-working space. He's about to reply telling her it will have to wait until next week when he scans the reset of the email chain and notices that Jeff and Kaito have already agreed to the meeting.

Great. Not a chance I can get out of this one now. He sends a terse reply back, agreeing to the meeting. *At least she didn't schedule it for the middle of the night! Looks like Kaito has drawn the short straw this time.* Then he turns his email notifications off and goes back to what he was working on, hitting the keys a little too hard as he types.

****

Sunita leans back in her chair and stretches, reaching her hands above her head and giving a little yawn. She's excited about the direction of the project and feels as though they're making real progress with the R&D. This is the reason she became a solar engineer. To make a difference. But she can only do so much and momentum is really building. She needs some help and she has a couple of partner organisations in mind.

After spending what felt like all the previous night thinking about how best to move the project forwards, she's decided that a meeting between herself, Adam, Jeff, Kaito and Dave is the only way to go. That's why she emailed them all first thing.

This morning she walked along the beach at Hout Bay, in Capetown, and stared out at the vastness of the ocean, marvelling at the consistency of the waves rolling in. By the time she was at her desk at 7.30 a.m., she knew she needed to send the email and meeting invite. It was early enough that Kaito was still online and, sure enough, he was the first to respond. She was surprised to see Jeff reply too – she must have caught him just before he went to bed.

Dave replied shortly after and, finally, Adam. She hadn't been able to tell if his reply was short because he was busy, or annoyed, or both. But they needed a discussion if they were going to make progress.

She takes a sip of water, then returns to her laptop. She's producing documents about the three organisations she'd like to work with on the R&D of their new solar project and she wants them to be ready in time for the meeting.

****

At 3.55 p.m. Adam settles himself in the small conference room at his co-working space. He opens Zoom and logs into the meeting. He composes himself. He knows what he needs to do – get this over with as quickly as possible so they can all move forward.

Sunita comes online and lets him into the meeting room, they've barely said hello when Dave also dials in. Then Jeff joins them from California. *He looks a lot livelier than I do at that time of the morning*, Adam thinks. Finally Kaito dials in, sitting at his computer with the soft glow of his screen and desk lamp illuminating his features. After the challenges of scheduling their initial calls, they have all agreed that they would have to take it in turns to be the one to get up in the middle of the night.

After everyone has exchanged pleasantries, Adam decides he needs to step in and take control of the meeting to keep it on track and as succinct as possible. 'Thanks for all getting together on such short notice,' he begins. 'I don't have lots of time today, so let's get started. Now, I've read through all the emails you've all sent me today and this is what I think we should do. . .'

He finishes his summary of where they're at and what the next steps are with the question, 'What do you think?' Adam is expecting everyone to agree, so he's a little taken aback when Sunita starts talking about her perspective on the R&D partners. He starts to interrupt her, to bring her back on track, when Kaito steps in, talking in his even and measured tone. 'We could certainly use the assistance. Sunita and I are reaching the limits of our collective scientific brain power.' Adam notices Sunita smile at this. 'Yes, but I've just outlined how we can move forward with the R&D,' Adam asserts, trying to hide the frustration in his voice, but not quite managing it.

Dave has said very little. He's taking everything in, listening to everyone and Adam knows that he'll have an opinion to share after he's had time to consider all that's been said. There's a pause with a tinge of awkwardness. Jeff manages a smile. 'I think it's great that Sunita initiated this call today. There are certainly a few things we all need to be in agreement on in relation to this project before we can take it forward,' Jeff says.

Adam can feel his frustration rising as Sunita, Jeff and Kaito continue with their back and forth. Dave even ventures an opinion. Adam glances at his watch. He's been on this call for over half an hour and they haven't resolved anything. He doesn't have time for this. 'I think we all agree this is an important decision. These are going to be our key partners for R&D and we want to get that right,' Adam cuts in. 'But I can't make a decision without all the information, so Sunita can you send me all the details you have about these companies, give me a week to go through everything and then we can catch up again?'

There's an awkward silence. 'Sure, I'll send the documents over this evening,' Sunita offers, sounding a little deflated. 'Great, thanks. And thanks for your time today, I'll speak to you soon.' Adam leaves the meeting. He looks at his watch. *45 minutes, that could have been worse.*

His thoughts are interrupted by his mobile ringing. He looks to his left, where his phone sits on the desk and sees that it's Jeff. With a slight feeling of unease, he answers, 'Hi Jeff.'

'Hi Adam,' Jeff says, 'I think we need to talk because I'm not sure you realise what you're doing to Sunita and the rest of the team by just bulldozing all the decisions.'

'What? It's my job to make the decisions, I'm the MD, the buck stops with me and these are important decisions to get right Jeff, you've got to agree with that?'

'Sure I do, but you've got to see this....'

'Look, Jeff, I don't have time to argue about this right now. I still have so much work to still do today and now I need to find time to read Sunita's reports.'

'This is exactly what I'm talking about Adam. You've got to let people finish. Do you have any idea of the impact that your behaviour is having on Sunita and the rest of the team? You don't always have to be the smartest person in the room.'

'I've got 25 years in this business, I know that making a bad decision at this stage could kill the company. I thought you'd appreciate the due diligence given that you're in finance.'

'That's not what this is about. But since you mention that, I think now is the time for moving quickly to grasp the big opportunities, not moving slowly. We'll miss out on much bigger things if we don't get involved with some of the partners Sunita has been researching. And she has researched them, Adam. She's done the due diligence. Trust her when she recommends them because she knows what she's talking about.'

'I'll make reading her reports my priority tomorrow,' Adam replies.

'Just think about what I'm saying, please. We can talk again tomorrow if you need to. I won't take up any more of your time now.' Jeff says.

They say goodbye and Adam hangs up. Part of him knows Jeff is right, and he does trust Sunita, but it's such a big decision. He exhales loudly. He knows he raised his voice in the meeting. Out of the corner of his eye he had noticed a few heads turning to look at him through the glass wall of the conference room during a particularly heated exchange. He sighs, turns back to his computer and sends a few more emails. He realises he's hitting the keys heavily now. *Time to go home. These will still be here in the morning.* Just as he's about to close his inbox, the reports from Sunita arrive. He flags them with a reminder for 8 a.m., closes his laptop and leaves the conference room, giving a terse nod and brief 'goodbye' to those still working at the desks in the co-working space.

****

When he arrives home Rose is in the kitchen preparing dinner. As he walks in she greets him with a smile, half shrouded in the steam from the pans on the cooker. 'Hi honey, how was your day?' she asks.

He hesitates, and Rose gives him a slight frown. 'Something wrong?' Adam sighs, slumps down at the table and relates the whole scenario of what happened in the meeting and his call with Jeff. Rose listens, occasionally stirring the sauce or adding salt to the pasta.

When Adam has finished venting, she walks across the kitchen and sits down next to him. 'Well, there was always going to be a transition period when you left the corporate environment for a startup,' she says. Adam sighs, 'I know, but I don't understand why everyone is being so difficult.'

Rose smiles. Adam loves her knowing smile. 'Maybe you need to look at this from a different perspective,' she says. Adam feels himself tensing up. That's what Jeff had tried to tell him too. 'But. . .' Rose reaches out her hand and touches his arm. 'Adam, I'm not attacking you, I'm just trying to help. Let me ask you a couple of questions, ok?'

He nods. Rose continues, 'I know that you think very highly of Sunita and we both know she always goes the extra mile. Just consider, will she keep doing that and putting in the extra effort if she thinks you don't trust her judgement and expertise? And what will everyone else on the team do if they think you don't trust them?'

She pauses, Adam nods. 'You also have to think about whether this is the best way to make decisions. You're keeping so much control at the moment and giving yourself so much extra work, but you have to think about whether this is the optimal way to approach the business. You don't have to answer me, but just think about those things, ok?' She smiles, squeezes his arm and goes back to the stove. Adam sighs and leans back. 'Thanks Rose,' he says. 'Now, what's for dinner? It smells delicious.'

****

By Monday, Adam has had time to relax. He gets up early to hit the gym before going to work and wading through his inbox. He's been mulling over what Rose said to him for a couple of days. *Maybe I do need to change my approach. What I'm doing clearly isn't working, so trying something different might be the answer. But what if that doesn't work? What if it makes things worse? But what if it makes them better?* It's been like a song on repeat in his head.

A heavy gym session always makes him feel better. At 6 a.m. it's still nice and quiet. The sun is up by the time he walks through the door, swiping his membership card and waiting for the barrier to open with a faint hiss. *Where has this year gone? It's late June already, it won't be long before Georgia is off to study in California.* Adam shakes his head and makes his way to the locker room. In the gym, he puts his headphones in, hits play on his workout playlist and gets stuck into his warm-up. By the time he's working through his weight sets, he's feeling good, better than he has for a while. The change in job has given him more time to work out and he's enjoying feeling stronger and fitter than he has in years. He's been building up his deadlifts and today he feels ready to add a little more weight.

He wraps his hands around the bar. He knows he's got his hands in the right place because the metal still feels slightly warm after his last set. He focuses, plants his feet, takes a deep breath in and with a strong exhale and a grunt, lifts the bar off the floor. He is surprised by how easy that felt. He drops the weights, enjoying the satisfying sound of them hitting the ground, even if not from a great height. He manages two more reps at this weight comfortably. Then he adds just a little more weight. Again, he plants his feet, creating a strong foundation. All his muscles work in unison with his breath and he lifts the heavier bar, posting a PB for the last five years. As he releases the weights to the floor, he suddenly understands what Rose meant. He trusts his muscles to do what they need to do. He needs to start letting his team do some of the lifting, especially when they want to.

****

In Part 1, I explained the three big rocks that comprise the head of the body. In Part 2, I'll be telling you about the three big rocks that comprise the dynamic part of the body – the skeleton and muscles. These three rocks are:

4. Meetings and agenda
5. Knowledge management
6. Regular feedback

In this chapter, I'll explain the agenda and knowledge management. By getting these two rocks in place, you will allow everyone in the team to contribute and shine. As you'll remember from Part 1, knowledge management should be linked to the strengths and talents of your team members.

When you're creating structured communication, you need to begin by having a regular forum. As you can see from part two of Adam's story, his company has got into the habit of having weekly team meetings for the leadership team.

Having structured communication like this is essential when you're managing virtual teams. This shouldn't be manager-centric or problem-centric, but an opportunity for everyone in the team to talk, voice their opinions and feel as though they're being heard.

I'd like to tell you a brief story to give you an insight into the importance of listening and empowering within virtual teams. In all the years I've spent studying, coaching and leading virtual teams, I've learned many important lessons. But I've also been a member of virtual teams, so I have a 360-degree view, and while I've learned important lessons from excellent leaders, I've also learned lessons from poor leaders. This story is about one of the poor leaders.

In fact, a fellow team member called him a 'waste of space', which might sound harsh, but was unfortunately fair. This leader did not apply several of the basics required for igniting global talent. I'll just share the top three things he did wrong:

1. *Top-down communication: We had weekly calls with the team, but our 'waste of space' did all the talking. His weekly agenda was the reports and directives from him. People were not encouraged to contribute. Despite the fact that we were a great team, people became disengaged.*

2. *Avoiding debate: As the team became disengaged, things started to go wrong and issues arose that needed to be tackled head on. But our 'waste of space' did not have the insight or the bravery to address the issues. He was afraid to confront the situation.*

   He sent emails and when people didn't respond he didn't chase them or escalate. He never just picked up the phone. When you asked him about these issues, he would lower his voice and try to avoid them. He was trying to sound more authoritative and confident, even though he wasn't making well thought-out decisions. He didn't ask questions, listen or encourage debate.

3. *He practiced self-centred, eco-centric leadership: Due in a large part to his bad leadership, the project was failing. But instead of adjusting and stepping up to lead the team and tackle the challenges, his priorities were self-centred activities. He arranged long lunches. He made calls to the airline to upgrade to business class. Everyone in the team knew this was happening.*

Lessons for igniting global talent

What can you learn from this 'waste of space' about how to better manage your virtual team? There are three key takeaways:

1. *Ignite your team knowledge and commitment through bottom-up communication: As a leader, you must encourage bottom-up*

communication. Your operations are spread around the world. Your talent is spread around the world. You can never have all the answers. You have to make the knowledge of the team available to the team. Doing so will motivate and engage the members of your team.

2. *Bravely seek and confront the debate: There will always be points of discussion, differing opinions, multiple opinions and pain points. That's reality in the actual and the virtual world. All of these are exacerbated in a virtual world, however, without the advantage of shared actual experiences and knowledge. To ignite virtual talent, a leader must be constantly on the lookout for where debate is necessary, and have the bravery to confront it.*

3. *Be a generous, magnanimous leader: Put your team, your team members and your goal first. It's karma. When the team sees and senses this, they will always go the extra mile both for the team and for you. In virtual teams, just as in actual teams, leaders who are self-centred are simply just a 'waste of space'.*

In the past I have led virtual teams with hundreds of people in them. In my last job, where I was head of IT services for Europe, the Middle East and Africa (EMEA), I had 15 direct reports, but 100+ people in the team. Whenever I was leading a new team, I would start with a face-to-face workshop. On the second day, I'd ask the whole team how often we should have a team conference.

Most people suggest once a month. But I always challenged my team members to start with one meeting a week and if that felt like too much then we'd change it accordingly. Initially, I would get 60–70% of the team attending each virtual meeting, but by the end of the first month this would increase to 90%. What's more, we would keep this level of attendance.

How to Maintain Engagement in your Regular Team Meetings

What's the secret, I hear you ask? The secret to creating this level of engagement in meetings isn't what you see or hear, but what you do.

This is where an agenda is crucial. You need to break down the agenda in such a way that everyone has their own slot to talk, which allows everyone to contribute and shine. In my last job, I initially started the conferences with what I called a global update, because I was part of the global leadership team. This is the equivalent of giving an update as the team leader.

In my role, I would receive a lot of emails. Any that were urgent, I'd forward straight to the team, or the relevant person on the team, but any that were more of an update, I would retain. During the team call, I would briefly present these emails and ask people to ask questions. I was giving them an opportunity to interact.

Once I'd given my update, I'd hand over to the team and each person would get two minutes to give a personal update, where they could share a highlight from their life that had happened since the last meeting. It might be hitting a personal best in a half marathon, or enjoying a nice Chilean red wine at the weekend. It's very personal, but no one should talk for longer than two minutes.

After everyone has had the chance to give their personal update, each person gets another two minutes to talk about the milestones they've achieved. It's important that everyone does this in a structured way and that they don't go into details.

Your time together online is precious and you need to use it effectively. That means each person should talk briefly about the milestones they've achieved and flag up any issues they are encountering. This is an opportunity to decide if there is something that the team needs to resolve.

This helps to foster the gravity within the team. It also means that people will be clear about whether they need to take any actions after the meeting. It might be that some of your team members need to get together separately to resolve an issue.

Always Have an Agenda

Every virtual meeting should have an agenda. This is key. The agenda and purpose of the meeting needs to be clear before you start, whether you're having a brainstorming session, a meeting for updates or a decision-making meeting.

Change the Format Once a Month

Once a month, the format of this meeting would change. It's important to explain that this doesn't mean you have an extra meeting, you are simply changing the format of your existing team meeting.

In this monthly meeting, the leadership team would take part and I would insist that they all join in by video conference. That might be inconvenient for some, depending on the spread of time zones within the team, but it's important that all of the leadership team join via video.

I would also invite all of the leadership team's direct reports, the so-called extended leadership team. In some businesses, that might mean you have over 100 people attending the meeting. By contrast, small and medium-sized businesses that don't have the same established hierarchical structure may decide to invite key partners or key stakeholders from other departments within the company.

At this call, everyone should be prepared to talk about their strategic goal and present where they have reached with it. This doesn't need to be detailed. It should just be a maximum of one page of notes, covering the project management milestone ticks, risks, issues and budget updates and so on.

Remember, each person sets their strategic goal based on their strengths during the exercise to create the project roadmap and sets the interdependent goals that I talked about in Part 1. There shouldn't be any micromanagement of these goals. In a virtual team, everyone owns the strategic goal that they choose.

Allow People to Ask Questions

In the monthly meeting that includes the extended leadership team, it's important to give people the opportunity to ask questions. But to ensure that no one is being interrupted, and to keep the meeting to the agreed agenda and length, I find it's best to encourage people to ask questions via chat, and at the end of the meeting allow 15 minutes to go through the questions that have come up. You may find that there are similar questions from different people that you can categorise and answer.

The Importance of Time Management

It's essential that you have someone to manage the time in the meeting to keep it flowing. As I said, I used to break it down so that everyone would have an equal slot. I used to nominate someone to be what I would call the Services Coordinator, who would manage the agenda and manage the time in the meeting.

Having strict time management gives you a structure where, even if you have the tendency to posture or dominate and speak most of the time, you're not able to take over the whole meeting.

This is how the highest-performing teams work. For example, at Google's Project Aristotle, they would share the time in meetings, with each team member given an equal amount of airtime for speaking.

It's also important to consider the length of the meetings. In the smaller team meetings, with a maximum of 10 to 15 people who are each giving a personal update as well as an update on their strategic goals, the meeting shouldn't last longer than an hour and a half. In exceptional circumstances, if there are questions that need to be answered, you could spend another five or ten minutes talking, but if you think you will need this extra discussion time make sure you ask who can attend if the meeting is extended and plan your timing accordingly.

In a meeting with up to 100 people, like the extended leadership team meeting I talked about having once a month, you wouldn't give personal updates. A meeting of this size should be limited to two hours long. This should be enough time for everyone to deliver a brief update on their progress with their strategic goal and for some Q&A.

No meeting should last longer than two hours, because at this point you hit a psychological barrier. Meetings that go on for longer than two hours, particularly online with participants based around the world, will feel cumbersome if they're too long. You also have to consider that in a global team, some people may be sacrificing time from their personal life to attend and you need to be mindful of this.

Making Time for Personal and Professional

This suggested structure for meetings includes time for people to talk about their personal lives as well as their professional work.

The monthly catchup with the extended leadership team is formal, with each person's update on their strategic goal being recorded. This means it's trackable.

In virtual teams it's important to make sure that every meeting isn't just about work though. That's why it's important to allow time to talk about personal updates in the weekly team meetings. Having formal and informal meetings is important to create that sense of cohesion within your virtual team.

Don't Have Too Many Meetings

While meetings are important for creating that gravity within your virtual power team, you should make sure that you don't schedule too many meetings. People are increasingly complaining that they spend all day in meetings and don't have time to produce results and cooperate within smaller groups. This has become a particularly common complaint following the Covid-19 pandemic.

However, if you have set your goals from the bottom up and each person has picked their goal based on their strengths, they will have taken clear ownership of that goal. This will give them, and the team as a whole, more freedom, which may mean you don't need to have such frequent update meetings.

You need to decide whether weekly, bi-weekly or monthly meetings are required within your team and your industry. Ask your team how often they believe you should meet. You can always reduce or increase the frequency of the meetings if you need to.

How Often Should Virtual Teams Meet in Person?

This is one of the most frequently asked questions when I speak at conferences. In this context, I'm talking about how often virtual teams should meet in person. My recommendation would be at least once a year.

There are several reasons why I believe this is good for the dynamic of the team. We all operate in yearly cycles naturally, so personally it makes sense. But we also operate in yearly cycles from a business perspective. This means you will have financial results to share and can use these to help set strategic targets.

Of course, being able to meet in person depends on whether you have the budget to do so. The Covid-19 pandemic is also expected to change the way in which we cooperate. But even if you are unable to meet face to face once a year, you can still recreate this kind of annual meeting online.

When I was speaking at a conference in Bali in 2019, I was talking to companies who had 1,000+ employees who all work remotely from their homes, cafes, or whatever location they find inspiring. One of the key things I learned from them is that, if everyone works remotely and you don't have an office, it is best to meet in person every six months.

Setting the Agenda for an Annual Meeting

Whether you are hosting this meeting in person or online, the agenda will remain the same.

Firstly, this is not an update meeting. You may review the results, but you should do so at a very high level. The more important element of this meeting is goal setting. As I explained in Part 1, goal setting is key and you should set them from the bottom up.

Going back to this conference in Bali, these fully virtual teams would meet every six months. Six weeks in advance of each of these meetings, the leadership team would get together to define the purpose of the meeting – usually this was to create product roadmaps – and exactly how they wanted it to flow. The aim is to ensure that this bottom-up process is followed and that the team is able to achieve the deliverables that are set.

The reason they typically focus on product roadmaps in these face-to-face meetings is that the product development process requires a lot of interaction and, although technology has improved, the experience of having everyone in the same room with all the available tools is still unbeatable.

While there is no single right answer as to how often you should get your virtual teams together, every six months is a duration that works for many multinational organisations.

> **Tip:**
>
> *Six-monthly product roadmaps*

To make the most of these six-month product roadmaps you need to:

- Set a clear agenda. This should be done six weeks in advance by the senior leadership team.
- Look forward, not back. These meetings should be about planning for the future, not conducting reviews of the past.
- Focus on facilitation and co-creation. The leadership team should design a clear facilitation structure that includes time for individual contribution, small group work, presentation, and integration and co-creation as a team. Micromanagement and top-down management is not an option. Facilitation and co-creation creates empowerment, commitment and fosters the gravity.

That said, as a result of the Covid-19 pandemic, many companies will need to simulate this environment using virtual tools. While it isn't exactly the same, it is possible to recreate every element of a live meeting, such as by sharing whiteboards, using features to visualise what's being discussed and formatting and managing the meetings in such a way that everyone is able to contribute.

6

Bridging Time Zones and Knowledge Management

Two weeks later, Adam feels calm as he prepares for the video conference with their new R&D partners. When he'd looked at the documents Sunita had sent over, he could tell she had done a great deal of research. He wasn't the only person on the team who was impressed. Dave, Jeff and Kaito had all voiced their support too; and although it was a joint decision over who to work with, the new partners were the three preferred by Sunita.

Adam dials into the call and waits for Sunita to let him in. He's five minutes early and she's ready and waiting. She greets him with a beaming smile. 'I'm so excited about this, I just can't tell you!' she says. He grins back. 'Me too. It's great that we're getting the project moving. I'll do the introductions once everyone is here, and then I'll hand over to you and Kaito to lead the rest of the meeting, just like we discussed, ok?' 'Perfect, oh, Kaito's dialling in now.'

Slowly but surely, all the other participants dial in. There are 27 of them on the call in total.

After introducing himself and the other members of their top team, Adam sits back and listens. He takes odd notes but mostly he just absorbs what's happening. Sunita leads the discussion masterfully. He's impressed by how she is able to steer everyone back on topic. Kaito plays a supporting role, but chips in with excellent insights. After an hour and a half, everyone has agreed on the next steps.

This time, Adam isn't the first to leave the meeting. He notices that Jeff, Kaito, Dave and Sunita have also remained online, waiting for the last of their partners to leave. 'That was awesome,' Sunita beams. 'I have a real mish-mash of notes to write up though – did anyone else take any notes on the call? I kept getting distracted so I have some gaps' 'I took a few,' Adam volunteers, 'But I'm not sure how much use they'll be.' 'I'm sorry, I only took notes on the financial side of things,' Jeff adds.

After a few more minutes of discussion, they realise that they've all noted down different aspects of the meeting. Kaito focused on recording the scientific queries and potential challenges ahead, while Dave made notes relating to the supply chain. They all agree to send their notes to Sunita, who will try to pull them together into a working document.

'This might be a challenge,' Sunita says. 'We might need another call, just to fill in any gaps.'

****

Over the coming week, keeping on top of all the documentation becomes more challenging. Each of the three new R&D partners are sending documents over and Sunita is struggling to keep on top of things.

Her email pings again and she almost doesn't want to look. Another email with another three attachments! She sighs. Spending so much time on the admin is pulling her focus from the research side of the project, the part she really loves. She opens the email and downloads the attachments, scanning each to work out which of her many folders these ones need to be saved in.

She reaches for her coffee mug, takes a sip and pulls a face. It's stone cold. She sighs, rises from her chair and heads to the kitchen to make a fresh cup. *I think I need to talk to the rest of the team about getting some help with the organisational side of the project. I'll mention it in our catch-up call on Wednesday.*

****

On Wednesday, no one disagrees that they need some organisational support, but the next challenge is finding someone who will fit in with the rest of the team. They've become so close in the past six months and are now working well together. They all agree that they need to hire carefully so as not to upset the dynamic.

They all go away and reach out to their networks. In the coming week, they each speak to people who could be right to take on the knowledge management role. One afternoon, Dave calls Adam.

'Hi Adam, do you remember the Bulgarian project manager who worked with us a few years back? Her name was Maya.'

'I think so, she was at the company for about six months if I remember rightly?'

'Yeah, that's it. She was part of that joint exploration project with the Nordic oil company. Anyway, I just heard through another contact that she's between jobs at the moment. What do you think? I remember her being really efficient.'

'Sounds like it could be worth a try. Why don't you set up a call with her, sound her out and see what you think, then we can go from there?'

'Great, I'll get in touch with her this afternoon.'

After a few LinkedIn messages, Dave and Maya arrange a call. They talk for almost an hour and when Dave gets off the phone he's happy. She's calm, organised and she knows the renewable energy sector, having transitioned to the industry not long after working on the project that Dave and Adam remember.

The following week, Dave sets up a video conference with the rest of the team to introduce Maya. They've all agreed that they need to meet her before they offer her the knowledge management and collaboration expert role. Dave is confident that she's the right fit though.

During the call, they all ask questions. Dave grins when he sees Sunita smile at Maya's mention of a digital filing system. After 45 minutes, Maya leaves the call. 'So, what do you think?' Dave asks. It's a resounding 'yes' from the rest of the team.

****

As Maya hits the 'Leave meeting' button, she's smiling. She knows she has to wait for a decision, but that felt like it went well. *They definitely need some help! Poor Sunita sounds like she's drowning in documents and proposals.* Maya takes a sip of her water, her hand absent-mindedly reaching for the leaves of the plant that she keeps on her desk. She often finds herself gently playing with them when she's thinking. *This could be a good move for me. I've been looking for a project that I'm passionate about and they are definitely going in the right direction.*

Her thoughts are brought back to the room by a 'ping' on her phone. It's a message from Dave: she's got the job! Maya grins broadly and claps her hands together. She's excited about getting started and she can't wait to get stuck into their documents – she loves the challenge of setting up a new filing system and getting everything in order.

****

In Maya's first two weeks on the job, it's blindingly obvious to her that no one has been properly keeping track of documents or meeting notes. She has several calls with Sunita, who does her best to explain how she's been attempting to file the mountain of paperwork she's been receiving. But it's clear that Sunita has been completely overwhelmed by what's come her way and hadn't expected to have so much to deal with.

Maya also receives photos of handwritten notes taken by Jeff and Adam in meetings. *Have they not heard of collaborative documents?* She sighs. It's all about priorities. Her first job is to organise what they have and find out what's missing, then she can start introducing the virtual tools that will make a world of difference going forward.

****

At Maya's first team meeting, during her first week with the company, she says very little and absorbs everything that is going on. She takes notes and sends them round to everyone afterwards. By the following week, she's ready to contribute more and to start to address some of the issues she's identified.

Towards the end of the meeting, Adam asks her how she's getting on with the knowledge management. It's the perfect opening.

'I'm making progress on the filing and we have a proper system in place now, but I'd like to talk to all of you about using some virtual collaborative tools to make all of our lives easier in future. I think it'll be essential, especially now that the work with the R&D partners is stepping up a notch.' She pauses.

'What did you have in mind?' Adam asks. Maya smiles. 'Quite a lot, actually. . .'

****

Adam is loading his car with bags and Georgia is bouncing around excitedly. 'I can't believe we're spending the whole weekend at the beach!' she squeals. Adam laughs. 'I hope you're not going to be bouncing around like that all the way in the car?!' Georgia fixes him with her best teenage stare, breaks into a grin and dashes back into the house. 'Mum, hurry up! The car's packed now. . .'

They've rented a beach lodge for the weekend and Adam is determined to take the weekend off. He's told the team that he'll be checking his emails first thing in the morning and last thing at night, but otherwise not to call him unless it's an absolute emergency. He leans back against the side of the car. *They've got this under control. Having Maya to organise everyone has made a world of difference and Sunita seems much happier than she was a few weeks ago.*

His thoughts are interrupted as he sees Georgia practically dragging Rose out of the house. 'I've got to lock up!' she says, and Georgia releases her mother's hand and races towards the car. Rose turns, grins at Adam, closes and locks the front door and joins them by the car.

By the following evening, Adam feels more relaxed than he has in years. They've spent the whole day on the beach. Chilly sea dips. Shoes filled with sand. Ice creams with flakes in them. That was the agenda for the day. Georgia was happy too because they were able to do a beach clean. He's simply enjoyed spending this time with her and Rose, and now he's sitting on the terrace of their beach lodge, watching the last glimmers of sunlight disappear behind the horizon. The sky is stained with a myriad of pinks and reds. Rose comes and snuggles next to him, handing him a glass of red wine. He puts one arm around her, takes a deep breath and just smiles.

****

One of the challenges when you have an international virtual team can be managing time zones. As we saw in Adam's story, it can be easy to schedule meetings for times that are inconvenient for other team members. But as we also saw in that story, it's important to acknowledge that sometimes you will need to be the person who gets up and dressed in the middle of the night.

When it comes to arranging your regular team meetings, whether they are weekly or monthly, you need to think about how this might affect some of your team members.

I will always give people the option to dial in by phone, rather than joining with their video. This is because when you have a big virtual team, people may not always be somewhere they can easily talk via video. For example, some of your team members may be at the airport just before a flight.

Or if it is early in the morning, being able to dial in by phone means they don't have to get fully dressed and put a suit on. They can participate in the meeting in their bathrobe if they really want to. In the informal, weekly calls I mentioned in the last chapter, it is important to give people this option so that they feel they are able to listen to what's going on and contribute.

If you need to have a video call, make sure you tell people ahead of the meeting to give them time to prepare. This is particularly important if they will be attending at an inconvenient time in their home country.

Finding the Optimum Time for Meetings

When you are managing a team spread across multiple time zones, think about how you can schedule meetings to be as convenient as possible. For instance, lunchtime in central Europe is also a good time for those who are based in Asia. Or if you have predominantly American participants, you would choose a time in the late afternoon or evening in Europe, as this would mean it will be morning in the Americas.

Tip:

The Golden Hour

In Central European Time (CET) 14:00–15:00 is known as the Golden Hour in many multinational organisations. This is because it falls in the evening for those working in the Asia-Pacific region, while it's first thing in the morning for those working in the Americas. The Middle East and Africa is typically within a couple of hours of CET too.

However, you will need to accept that, in a global team, any meeting you schedule is likely to be inconvenient for somebody.

Coping with Language Barriers

Other issues you may have to consider within a global team are language barriers and challenging accents. While you will more than likely share a common language, sometimes it can be difficult to understand someone or, if that language isn't your native tongue, you might simply miss something.

One of the best ways to reduce the impact of any language barrier is to use the chat function in your online conferencing software. In fact, I would recommend that you have someone during the meeting who summarises any discussion in the chat. They should also record the decisions and key outcomes in the chat.

If you have questions, and particularly if you aren't a native speaker, I would recommend that you write down your question and send it through the chat at the same time that you speak it.

Pay attention to who is speaking and make sure that everyone contributes to the meeting. If you have some introverts on your team, or maybe people who feel as though their language skills aren't good enough, encourage them to speak. They will all have great talents and you want to make sure that their talents are brought into the team.

If somebody hasn't spoken for a while, ask for their opinion. You'll more than likely be surprised by the quality of their input.

One of the key distinctions between a high-performing team and a group of people who collaborate virtually is that the high-performing teams have an equal share of airtime. It's unlikely that this will happen naturally to begin with, so make sure you instigate it and encourage those who haven't spoken to contribute.

When someone who hasn't contributed much to the meeting introduces a good idea, make sure you praise them. This will not only make them feel good and encourage them to contribute more in future, but it will also encourage everyone in your team to share their ideas.

To break the ice, especially when a team is new to working together, you should encourage meta-communication. What I mean by this is talking about mutual feelings, the team's common goals and the interdependent goals that you set. Ask questions about the team's why. By asking these questions and discussing these areas, you will create a common understanding and foster an atmosphere that encourages people to speak up, even if they are feeling nervous about a perceived language barrier.

How to Deal with Challenging Accents (And Make Sure Everyone is Understood)

If you've worked in a global team, chances are you will have had at least one colleague whose accent you struggle to understand sometimes. Maybe when they get emotional or excited and start speaking quickly, you struggle to understand them. Even if you are a native speaker of your team's common language, don't forget that others may struggle to understand your accent. Be mindful of this.

Here are some top tips to make sure that everyone is understood in a meeting.

Speak Slowly

My first tip is to speak slowly and use globally understood English. If you are a native speaker, articulate very clearly and consciously slow down your speech.

Use Visuals

Use pictures, visual aids and slides. If you can use a picture to clarify your words rather than using text on a slide, then do it. Avoid using idioms and be aware of any jargon that might not be familiar to non-native speakers.

Check Everyone Understands

Throughout a meeting, regularly check understanding. It is your responsibility to be understood, so every now and then ask if everyone understands. You could ask them to rephrase what you've just said and consider capturing this on the chat.

Repeat and Summarise

When you make a statement, or come to a decision, repeat the essence of what you've discussed and put this in the chat. If you have someone who is managing the agenda, you may decide to ask them to capture the key decisions and aspects from a meeting and put it in the chat channels. This will help non-native speakers, because they can read as well as listen.

Put Questions and Statements in Writing

Use the chat function, as I mentioned above, when you're asking questions or summarising key decisions. This will help to ensure everyone understands what you are asking or saying and will be particularly helpful for those who are non-native speakers of the language.

Ask if you Don't Understand

If you are listening to someone else and don't understand what they're saying, don't be afraid to ask for clarification. You are unlikely to be the only person who doesn't understand, especially if there is a mix of native and non-native speakers in your group.

Use Humour

As well as visual aids, use humour to keep your team engaged. Not every image you use needs to explain something, it could just be a way of introducing some humour to the meeting.

Make Use of Different Tools

Sharing tools are invaluable for virtual teams. You can use them to encourage collaboration and to ensure that everyone understands what is happening in a meeting. Share the agenda before the meeting and consider whether you want people to be able to edit the agenda before the meeting. If that's the case, share it via an appropriate tool, such as Google Drive.

Use the chat functionality wisely and make use of virtual whiteboards to facilitate brainstorming and the simultaneous sharing of ideas. You can even use voting tools to get immediate feedback on ideas or decisions.

The key is to ensure that you're using the right tool for the right purpose and that you establish rules within the team about which tools are used for which purposes. This will help you visualise and bring clarity to your meetings.

Agree on a Channel for Urgent Communication

When your team works in different locations and in different time zones, it's essential that you decide on a channel that can be used for urgent communication.

I once worked with a German automotive company that had production facilities in Mexico. The German managers of the company were becoming annoyed that they'd receive a voicemail at around 10 p.m. In Germany, this is considered a sacred time for family. Leaving a voicemail on someone's mobile phone also means that you require an urgent response in Germany.

When I looked into this particular issue, I quickly discovered that in Mexico voicemails aren't perceived as urgent. There was simply a difference in understanding between people from the two countries.

To solve this issue, the team decided to use one particular text messaging service – in this instance WhatsApp – for urgent communication. Everybody committed to checking this channel every two hours and they also agreed that there would always be a response within two hours, even if it couldn't be a complete response to an issue. By this I mean that someone would acknowledge the issue and tell them they would respond in the morning, for example.

It's important that the team decides not only which channel to use, but also on what the response time should be, especially if you have people working in many time zones.

Knowledge Management

Knowledge management within your team is one of the three big rocks that makes up this part of the body. When you're hosting virtual meetings with your team make sure that everyone has their email and notifications turned off so that there are no distractions.

You want to make sure that everyone can focus on the discussion and collaborate effectively. I talked in the last chapter about the importance of setting an agenda, so use this to help everyone focus.

When you're collaborating in an online meeting, ensure that all of your team members are working on the same document. Don't send attachments, send links to documents that you are all able to edit in real time. Platforms such as Google Drive and Dropbox are ideal for this purpose.

Whenever possible, you want to have a single source of knowledge. You want to avoid having multiple documents that need to be combined into one, or multiple versions of the same document. By using digital collaboration tools, you can avoid any issues with someone having an out-of-date version of any given document.

There are three key elements to consider in relation to knowledge management.

Key Topics

The first is to decide on the key topics that are relevant to your team. As with other decisions, this should be a team effort. You shouldn't dictate these key topics from the top down, but should encourage your team to decide on them from the bottom up.

The best way to do this is to collate everyone's thoughts on what the key topics should be and to vote on the ones that are relevant to the team. Once you have determined your team's key topics, link these to key subject matter areas and to the expertise of the people within your team.

Allow people to choose their focus based on their strengths. This is particularly important for any subject-area experts. Allow them to own each of these areas. They will be the custodians of that knowledge and the ones to drive the creation of fresh, new content and discussion around the theory.

Think back to Adam's story and how much better the team operated once he gave Sunita and Kaito the freedom to use their subject-area knowledge to lead from the front.

The Right Tools

The second element is having the right tools to allow people to share their work or thoughts and for others to immediately comment or contribute. Again, look at how Adam has allowed Kaito and Sunita to work together, outside of the key leadership team.

Setting up closed groups for subject-area experts, where they are free to collaborate and share ideas can really help with the development of those ideas. A closed Facebook group may be one tool you'd like to explore, because in here people can receive immediate feedback.

These are dynamic tools, where you share immediate feedback and comments, and then carry on with your work.

But it's also important to have static content that's produced using tools that are auditable. By this I mean that there needs to be version control so that you can see who has changed what, and when.

You can still collaborate in these documents, but you are storing information and you need to have an audit-controlled version. This should be the kind of document that people can always refer to. It's what I describe as a single source of the truth.

Give People Ownership but Always Give Feedback

You need to make sure that you give your team members ownership of this knowledge. You can link this ownership – these knowledge custodians, as I like to call them – to people's strengths.

As a manager, it's important that you engage with the various tools your team is using. Send likes and leave positive comments because this will nurture the feedback culture within your team, which I'll talk more about in the next chapter.

Whatever tools you're using to capture your knowledge, make sure you have owners, custodians, based on their strengths. It's essential that you have both dynamic content and tools that allow for quick feedback, as well as systems where you can have a single source of the truth.

Encourage People to Join a Community

If you have several hubs in different countries around the world – satellite members of your team – or if you decide that you want to have a completely remote team, you need to consider how you can help everyone to feel as though they belong.

Based on my experiences of working with people who have worked remotely for years, having a place of belonging is important because after a time, working remotely can be tough.

I once worked with an event business, where the two founders decided to become digital nomads and moved the whole team to a remote structure. They got rid of their office so the other eight people in their team could work from wherever they wanted, whether that was at home, in a coffee shop or somewhere else.

Once a week the two founders held an online meeting with everyone in the team, but after just two months of working remotely, two of the key members of the team left the business. They weren't having enough fun and they were missing the in-person interaction.

The point is that working online long term isn't suitable for everyone. It's key for any remote worker to be self-motivated. You can help people who aren't naturally self-driven in this way to thrive as remote workers if you focus on their empowerment, through the interdependent goals, giving them ownership of their work and a lot of recognition, as I discussed in Part 1.

If you don't have an office, make sure that your people are grounded in their local communities. Co-working spaces have really helped, because people can work in an office-type environment, they get to have this interaction and feel like they're part of a community.

If there isn't a co-working space in your city, look for other ways you can engage in local communities. There may even be a way that your organisation can support this.

Build Regional Zonal Communities

If you have team members spread within different regions of the world, such as the Asia-Pacific, Europe, the Middle East, Africa and the Americas, explore hosting regional meetings if your budget will allow.

This enables people who work together and talk online all the time to finally meet in person. You can still build regional zonal communities without meeting up in person, and this is likely to be something more businesses explore due to the Covid-19 pandemic.

I have been involved in fantastic webinars and Zoom experiences where we as a team are co-creating, sharing and imagining the future. These experiences are created by the design of the meeting and the online experience. With proper planning, you can make these meetings as emotionally charged as in-person events.

This is about having a team bonding experience, so make sure that you allow for meetings that aren't just about reviews and updates. Explore how you can incorporate these kinds of emotional meetings and develop a sense of community within your remote teams.

Best Practice for Online Communication

To get the most out of these online meetings, I'll share some of the best practices relating to online communication that I've collected over the years.

Be the First to Turn your Camera on

Visual communication helps a lot and we all know that body language has a bigger impact on communication than simple words. By switching your camera on, you open the channel. Although you can't see someone's full body, you can see facial expressions and you can gesticulate. This can help you to make the experience much closer to the live one. If you do it first, people will follow.

Set an Agenda

I talked about this in the previous chapter, but it's essential to set a clear agenda. Only invite people to the parts of the meeting that are relevant and try to minimise the time spent in meetings. Agendas are a must for any meeting, but they're even more important for virtual meetings. No agenda, no meeting.

Set your Camera up at Eye Level

If you just have your camera on your desk and you're looking down into it, it can be a bit intimidating. Where possible, try to have your webcam at eye level and look directly into the camera.

Use Headsets to Improve Voice Quality

Make sure that the quality of your sound is good. Headsets can be especially useful for longer meetings.

I'd like to close this chapter by telling you a humorous story about dealing with new technology, the unexpected and bad luck, in relation to online meetings.

The new online tools like Zoom, Slack, Skype, and many more, help us to move faster and smarter. But working with new tools can sometimes bring unique challenges. In 2012, Tim, a colleague of mine, and I were working on a project out of a hotel in Almaty, Kazakhstan.

We had a conference call planned with a large team. But there was no wifi in the hotel and I was struggling to dial in from the landline. Using my mobile wasn't really an option as it cost a fortune. Tim had a local KZ sim card and we agreed that I would join him in his room at the hotel for the call.

He wanted to take a quick shower before the meeting. I had to return to my room to pick up my laptop, so he gave me the key to his room.

Before I returned with my computer, I wanted to give Tim some warning that I was about to let myself in, so I sent him what I thought was a private message saying 'Tim, are you still naked? I'm coming!'. However, I sent it to the public chat, not realizing that Tim and many of our colleagues had already dialled into the call.

Message to Everyone: 'Tim, are you still naked? I'm coming!'

You can imagine the reaction from the rest of the team! 'Tim, are you naked? Can you turn on your video? No, on second thoughts don't!' and so on. To this day, Tim and I still receive comments about this call.

> **From Me to Everyone:**
>
> Tim, are you still naked? I'm coming!'

But what should you do if you're struggling to dial in? Firstly, put a message in the public chat (and make sure you know that it's the public chat). There are some other lessons you can take from my story:

- *Know when the call starts*

- *Be careful what you shout/put in the chat, particularly if it is sent to everyone*

- *Luck and fate are also factors you can't ignore.*

7

Regular Feedback

In addition to introducing regular team catch-ups, Adam has recently introduced individual feedback sessions with each team member too. He looks out of the office window to see clear blue sky. It's warm and he's hoping to fit another beach trip in before the summer is over, and before Georgia travels to California for her exchange trip in September.

He can't believe how quickly the year is going. Since choosing their R&D partners, the business has been growing rapidly. Sunita and Kaito have been busy dealing with all the technical aspects of the project and their hard work is beginning to pay off. Now that they've got a manufacturer in China, things will really take off.

Adam checks the time, takes a sip of water and then dials into the Zoom meeting with Sunita. He leads the meeting, barely giving Sunita a chance to get a word in edgeways. He's running through the list of things he wants to feed back to her. He's broadly pleased with how the R&D is going, but feels like some of the people in the partner organisations are running off on their own agendas and he wants Sunita to rein them in. He's happy to see how her relationship with Kaito has developed.

He's talked almost solidly for half an hour and he's reached the end of his list. 'Is there anything you wanted to discuss with me?'

'Actually, yes, there are a couple of things,' Sunita hesitates. 'I think we need to talk about a couple of the points you raised before. I didn't really get a chance to explain my side of it,' she begins. 'Oh, right, yeah,' Adam says, as though he's only just realising that Sunita might not blindly agree with everything he's said.

'But before we go back to that, I just wanted to say that I think we need to change up the structure of these feedback meetings. You're great at motivating me, and all of the team, to push forward with the project, but sometimes it feels as though you forget to listen to us,' she pauses, waiting for a response.

Adam starts to respond, 'I'm not sure that's entirely fair. . .' Then he pauses. He remembers Rose telling him to trust his experts, to allow them to take the lead sometimes. He takes a deep breath. 'Ok, was there anything else you wanted to tell me?'

Sunita smiles. 'Oh, right, yes, we've had a breakthrough with the R&D, in terms of one of the new materials we've been exploring. The short version is that there's an opportunity for a joint venture with an NGO that's affiliated with one of our R&D partners. I think it could really help us take the business to the next level, and it could also lead to an opportunity to diversify from solar to wind. I mean, there's a lot to consider, but to me this seems like a natural fit.'

Adam is surprised and feels a little blindsided. *Where did this come from?* Rose's voice drifts into his thoughts. *Adam, you have to trust your team. Give them a chance to lead.* He's suddenly aware that Sunita is waiting for a response from him. 'That sounds exciting. Can you send me the details so I can have a look?' He pauses, 'Actually, send the details to the whole team. This is the kind of decision we should all be involved in.'

'Absolutely,' Sunita says enthusiastically. 'I'll put together a report and send it round on Monday. Then we can discuss it in next week's team meeting.'

'Brilliant,' Adam says. They go back over a couple of Adam's earlier points, and then end their call. Adam sits for a moment, staring at his computer screen. A joint venture, already. *This could really push us to the next level.*

****

At the meeting the following week, everyone is enthusiastic about the proposal, especially Jeff who is convinced that he can easily raise the financial backing they need from Chinese investors and the Silicon Valley venture capitalists.

They decide to press ahead, and within a matter of months are named among the fastest growing startups in Silicon Valley. They're all riding high on the success of this first joint venture. Jeff is keen to start exploring diversification into the wind energy sector and the rest of the team agrees. There's a real sense of purpose and optimism driving them all now. During the most recent meeting Adam finds himself marvelling at what they've accomplished. *We've come so far in such a short space of time. We truly are making a difference now, in a good way.*

He can't wait to tell Rose and Georgia about their latest plans.

****

As he walks through the door he's greeted by the most delicious smell coming from the kitchen. With Georgia leaving for California in just a week, they've been working their way through her favourite meals and tonight is one of Adam's favourites too: Thai green curry, although of course Georgia insisted it was with tofu.

He shouts a quick hello before heading upstairs to change. When he walks into the kitchen he feels like he's walking on air. He can't wait to tell them about his day. Rose instantly notices that he's in a good mood. 'Why are you so happy?' she asks. Georgia looks up from her phone. 'Yeah Dad, you're grinning like a crazy person.'

Adam laughs. 'I've got some big news from work. . .' he says and proceeds to tell them all about how well the joint venture is going and how this has opened up an opportunity to diversify into wind, with a project in South America.

As he's talking, he notices that Georgia is frowning. He pauses, 'Georgia, what's wrong? I thought you'd be just as excited about this as I am?'

'It's just that, with those huge wind turbines, they can have such a negative effect on birds and their migratory patterns. I mean, we were learning about it in one of our lectures this week, and they don't even really know how it affects them in some parts of the world, because they've done so little research. I guess I'd just prefer it if you stuck to solar. You guys are doing so well with that, why do you want to change?'

Adam looks at Georgia, he feels deflated. 'Look, Georgia, we're going to do all the right environmental surveys and everything before a single turbine goes anywhere near the site. But I can see how much this means to you, so I'll go back to the team and tell them we should slow things down until we can properly explore all the impacts, ok?' Georgia nods.

'We've been learning about some projects where companies put profits before the environment, even when they're supposedly "green" initiatives, and they end up doing a lot of harm. That's all,' Georgia explains. 'If you're an environmentally friendly business, it just doesn't make sense to put your profits before the planet.' She gives Adam a half smile. He smiles back and sighs, 'As usual Georgia, you're right.' Rose gives his shoulder a gentle squeeze as she crosses the kitchen. 'Dinner's ready,' she says, 'Who's hungry?'

Adam is suddenly reminded of how delicious dinner smells. He cracks into a broad smile. 'I'm starving!' As they sit down to eat, his mind comes back to what Georgia said. *Planet before profits. I'm sure it's something we all agree with, but I'm not sure how happy the team will be about changing direction at this stage, especially Jeff.* He shuts off his inner monologue. *That is a problem for Monday.* And tucks into the steaming bowl of Thai green curry and jasmine rice that Rose has handed to him.

****

The next big rock is providing regular feedback. There is one aspect that is very important to this particular rock, which is what I'll start with.

It's essential that you don't criticise people in public and particularly not during an online call. That's because you will usually record these calls to share them with any team members who were unable to participate. If you need to share a criticism with someone, hold your horses and do it immediately after the call, with the person or people who you need to speak to.

Remember in Part 2 of our story that Jeff didn't criticise Adam in front of the team but instead chose to call him privately to deliver his criticism of Adam's behaviour? This is how you also need to react.

If you criticise someone publicly, and it's also recorded, it multiplies the impact this criticism can have. Because people are working virtually, they aren't always able to immediately discuss it together and, as a result, this can have a demoralising effect.

This is why this chapter is called Regular Feedback. This isn't just about criticising ad hoc, this is about creating a structured and regular platform for delivering performance feedback.

Giving this kind of feedback at regular intervals is essential. It should never just be sporadic. When I was managing a large team, I used to hold monthly calls with each one of my direct reports that were performance feedback sessions. Many companies do what they call performance reviews or appraisals once a year, often linking them to the bonus structure. But, in my opinion, feedback needs to be given much more frequently.

Of course, people will have annual targets, but now they also have their interdependent goals to work towards and they need feedback on how they're progressing towards their targets. These sessions would typically last for around an hour, sometimes slightly less or slightly more.

How to Structure a Performance Feedback Session

Start by talking about the positive things that your team member does. Appreciate their efforts and recognise what they do well. If you have some critical feedback which isn't urgent, you could provide it here in a constructive way. There is a whole methodology of giving feedback, which I'm not going to go into here. But if you would like to learn more, please feel free to get in touch.

One of the most important things to remember when you're having these performance feedback sessions is that it shouldn't just be a one-way street. If all you do is give feedback to the person in your team and they just receive it, this isn't a smart investment of your time.

Ask questions at the end of the session, such as:

- How can I help you?
- How can I be a better manager?
- What can I do to be a better manager?

You can find more creative ways to phrase these questions, but this is the gist. What you are doing is asking questions to get feedback about your performance. This is a sacred space, one-to-one, which creates trust. Listen to what people tell you and make sure you act on it, because otherwise you will lose your credibility.

Asking for and taking feedback on board as a manager is another way in which you can create strong bonds with your team members. These bonds are part of the gravity that holds your virtual team together, and this translates into improved performance the stronger the gravity becomes.

Learn the Difference Between the Development Plan and Performance Feedback

A development plan focuses on your professional development aspirations. You might aspire to a leadership role, becoming a senior manager or moving into a position of greater technical expertise.

As a leader, you should agree an area for development with each member of your team. Ask which area they would like to develop within the year and agree on some measures to help them achieve this. That might be training, on-the-job coaching or even just having the opportunity to work on a more challenging project.

In addition to agreeing on the overall aspiration, also agree on the specific skills they'd like to develop and make sure that you review their progress regularly. You may not need to review this as frequently as once a month, but you can set specific meetings to look at each team member's development plan. I would recommend doing this twice a year. The point is that your team will appreciate that you're investing in their professional development and this, too, translates into trust.

Many big corporates have a development planning process that is managed by the global HR department, but if you are a small business you should take the time to set this up for your team. You'll notice greater commitment and balance from them if you do.

Exercise

Find a partner, maybe at home or a colleague at work. Ask them to start speaking about one of their projects – this could be something as simple as their plan for their next holiday or what they intend to do at Christmas, for example.

After every statement that your colleague or partner makes, say: 'Yes, but. . .' and then provide a counter argument as to why what they're suggesting won't work or why it's not such a good idea. They will probably respond with another argument, and you should follow this with, 'Yes, but. . .' and then another counter argument.

Do this three or four times and then stop. See what happens, check in on the emotional levels of both yourself and your partner. I can already tell you that your partner will be frustrated and won't be feeling empowered. There are a few people who get fired up when they're challenged like this, but the majority will feel discouraged and won't want to continue the conversation.

Repeat this exercise again, with the same partner, and change the way you respond to their ideas. This time, after each statement they make say, 'Yes and. . .' and voice your support or introduce praise. The key is to just agree with what's being said and to use your creativity to support your partner. Do this for three or four iterations and notice what happens.

Ask your partner how they feel. You'll be amazed at the difference. People feel their imagination expanding and sometimes they will even feel smarter just by virtue of having been seen and encouraged.

Why is this so Important in Virtual Teams?

If, as a manager, you constantly respond with 'yes, but. . .' to the ideas your team have then they will contribute less, share fewer ideas with you and ultimately this will have a negative impact on the whole team's performance.

It's particularly noticeable in brainstorming sessions, where people will share their idea, make their statement and share their opinion too early and then sit back. There will already be distance because of how ideas have been received in the past. It doesn't encourage people to enrich each other's ideas.

Practice Generous Listening

The process of saying 'Yes. . .' and allowing the conversation to continue is called generous listening. It's about not cutting the conversation short. You'll no doubt have heard the saying 'We have two ears and just one mouth, so we should listen more and talk less.'

If you say, 'Yes, but. . .' immediately then you kill the conversation. I would encourage you to go through three or four rounds of just saying, 'Yes, and. . .' If you still need to kill the conversation or idea later you can, but let the person talking to you expand on their point first.

As a manager, this will improve the bond you have with your team members. You may also find that once someone has expanded on an idea, you're more receptive to it and may even change your mind about it.

What's more, if you adopt this 'Yes, and. . .' approach, the conversation will expand like magic. People feel smarter, they feel appreciated and you will find that your team have many more ideas for new projects, new products and other innovations in the future.

The most basic and powerful way to connect with another person is to just listen. Perhaps the most important thing we ever give to each other is our attention. Generous listening can change the level of contribution within your team and the quality of your team's ideas.

Use the Magic Words

'Yes, and. . .' is a simple and powerful way to listen and encourage people to share. But I'll give you four magic words that will always fuel the conversation, no matter how unappealing an idea might sound:

'Interesting, tell me more. . .'

I encourage you to try it and see the results.

There are a number of other phrases you can use for generous listening, including:

- That's a great idea!
- Can you talk more about that?
- What would that make possible?
- What else?
- What would that allow for?
- Help me understand...

Try to avoid asking 'How?' and 'Why?' at this stage. They aren't bad questions but they require more critical thinking, whereas asking 'What?' fuels creativity more effectively.

The most important thing is to focus on asking open questions and not restricting the conversation. An open question will require a full response of at least a sentence, not just 'Yes' or 'No' answers.

Speak About Possibilities

It's often common within virtual teams for people to simply focus on executing the tasks that they're given and to put less thought into possibility.

One very empowering question that can encourage this focus on possibility is: 'What seems impossible today, but if it were possible, would transform your work, team, business and company for the better?'

Start by asking yourself this question. Think about it for a little while and you will be surprised by the opportunities that open up.

Ask this question of your virtual team. Use a shared whiteboard so people can give their answers simultaneously, much like in a brainstorming session. You'll be amazed by the quality of the answers you receive. Then you can start building on each other's ideas, opening up the possibilities and breaking down the barriers.

Virtual does not mean your job is only about task execution. You can brainstorm and co-create together.

Tips for Sharing Team Feedback

If you're able to invest the time and have the budget to get together physically in the same place as a team, then you need to use this time wisely. But even if you invest a few half days to work intensively together as a team online, you should use this opportunity to share team feedback.

One format that I've found works well is: Continue Doing – Stop – Start.

Firstly, give each person on your team time to prepare feedback for every other team member. For each person, they should have three pieces of feedback and these should be delivered in the following order during the session:

1. Continue Doing: This should be something that the other person does well, that you appreciate, and you're asking them to do more of it. This is a good place to start because it

makes people feel that their efforts are appreciated and valued by the team.

2. Stop: In this part you would ask the person to stop doing particular behaviours or actions. Often you find these are things that they do with good intentions, but they aren't actually supporting the team. You're sharing blind spots with that person and helping them understand how they can better support the rest of the team.

3. Start: Finally, you return to a positive by outlining something that you believe the person is capable of, that they have the potential to do well, and ask them to start doing it to make the team even stronger.

Sit in a circle and get everyone to give their feedback for one team member, then move on to the next and so on until everyone has received feedback from the rest of the team. You can also do this virtually via a Zoom call, or another video conference.

The key is to not get defensive. If you have questions about something, or don't understand what someone means, you can ask clarification questions, but you shouldn't respond with a defensive statement, like 'I disagree...'. You need to listen and absorb the feedback that you're given.

Once everyone on the team has received feedback, you'll find that they have strengthened their bonds. For some, it might bring a show of sympathy, but because the focus is more on positives and what your team members appreciate about you, it will make you more dedicated. Encourage people to take the 'Stop' feedback as a reflection of what they can do to better support the whole team. This is an area for improvement and we all have those.

Taking time for self-reflection as a team will really help you to develop and build your virtual power team.

The Formula for a Virtual Power Team

As a mathematician, I can't resist a formula and there is one that I believe explains what you need for a virtual power team.

Virtual Power Team = $(P+V+I)/S$

P stands for personality
V stands for vision
I stands for intimacy
S stands for self (or ego)

When you create a virtual power team, you can work with the best experts in the world, but having the best experts doesn't necessarily lead to success. You need to unite them into a strong team. We all know from experience of watching sports, for instance, that the all-star teams seldom win the championship.

This is where your common vision comes in. This is all about having those common goals, that you set bottom-up like I discussed in Part 1.

Intimacy is the component that virtual teams most often neglect, but it's key. You need to encourage people to understand one another as human beings. Encourage them to dig deep. Use the formats like those that I shared in Part 1 of the book: creating a lifeline, the Strengths Matrix, the two-minute personal updates in meetings. All of this helps to build intimacy despite distance.

If you are able to meet in person once a year, use this opportunity for fun. Stay out late and work to deepen the intimacy between your team members.

We divide these three things by self or the ego, which means you want to have as little of the S in the formula as possible. In many corporate environments, senior managers will have hidden agendas that focus on something that facilitates their career. But if you set the agenda and goals as a team, as I discussed earlier in this part of the book, each individual will have their own interdependent goal. By being happy with the interdependent goal that you've chosen, you'll diminish the ego in the equation.

By following this formula, you'll be able to create a strong and motivated virtual power team.

Key Takeaways on Feedback

There are a few key takeaways from this chapter relating to feedback in a virtual setting.

Don't Criticise People in Public

I will go into this in more detail in the next chapter, but it's essential to avoid criticising people in a meeting, because this has a demoralising effect. Instead, do it immediately afterwards in a one-to-one call.

Use Face-to-Face Meetings for Team Feedback

On the rare occasions that you're able to all meet in person, use that time wisely. This is the ideal opportunity for a team feedback session, like I discussed above, using the Start – Stop – Continue Doing process.

Establish Regular One-to-One Meetings

Make sure you're having regular one-to-one meetings with your team. This is the chance to deliver performance feedback, but remember not to make it all about them. Ask how you can be a better boss and how you can provide more support to ensure that you're developing too.

8

Cross-Company Cooperation and Coopetition

Adam spends the whole weekend thinking about what Georgia has told him. After dinner, he takes his laptop into his study and spends a couple of hours doing some research into the impacts of large-scale wind farms on migratory birds. A part of him hopes that Georgia is exaggerating and that he'll be able to find the proof he needs to convince her, and himself, that everything will be okay.

But, of course, all he finds are more questions than answers and, with a heavy heart, he realises that Georgia is right and that if they truly are going to call themselves an environmentally responsible company, they will need to approach this differently.

On Monday, Adam wakes early, grabs his gym kit and heads out of the door before 6 a.m. He needs to clear his head. At this time of the day, the gym is mostly full of other professionals who like to work out before getting started on their morning. Headphones in, Adam starts on the treadmill to warm up. As his body starts to move and his legs pick up speed he begins to feel better. *It'll be okay, they'll understand.* He ups the tempo on the treadmill. *I'm sure they'll understand.* He's not sure if he believes it though. There are those niggling doubts returning to his mind.

He's working up a sweat now and can feel his heart rate climbing. *Is that because of the running or because of this meeting?* He increases the pace of the treadmill once more, sprinting for the final 30 seconds. Breathing heavily, he starts to slow to a walk, loosening up and getting ready for the next stage of his workout. Although his body has slowed down, his mind is working overtime. *How can I convince them? What do I need to do to show that this is the right thing to do for the business and the planet?*

In the weights room, Adam wants to work on his bench press but he needs someone to spot him. He looks around and notices one of the gym's PTs tidying dumbbells in the corner. Popping his headphones out of his ears he walks over. 'Excuse me, do you mind spotting me while I work on my bench press?' 'No problem,' the young man replies, 'Just give me a minute to finish up over here.' Adam nods, 'I'll go and set my bar up.'

He loads on weights, deciding that he'll build up to his one-rep max today and see if he can surpass it. He stacks a couple of extra plates at the end of the bench, ready to be added to the bar. The first reps come easily and he quickly finds his form. As the weight increases, he's having to push harder but he's far from reaching maximum effort. He smiles inwardly as the young PT looks impressed as he adds another 10kg to the bar.

Although he's focusing on lifting weights, another part of his brain is still ticking over the issue of the wind project. As he pushes up on what is now his heaviest bench press ever, he almost feels as though he's not going to get there. One last piece of effort sees him straighten his arms. He's pleased now that the PT's hands are hovering just below the bar, ready to help him lower.

His muscles are pumping and he needs assistance to prevent the bar landing across his chest. As he sits up, he smiles at the young man, 'Thanks for your help,' he says. 'My pleasure, it's always great to see someone hit an SB,' he smiles. 'Do you need help with anything else today?' *Just a monumental problem around wind farms and migratory birds…* 'No, thank you, I'm all set.' 'Great, I'll leave you to the rest of your session.'

As the PT walks across the room, and gets waved over by another member looking for a spotter, Adam suddenly realises what he needs to do. *I can't solve this alone, but I don't have to.*

****

When Adam arrives at the office less than an hour later, a plan has formed in his mind. He won't call an emergency team meeting today, he'll talk to the team on Wednesday, in their usual catch-up. He's aware that he will need some support though and he's keen to get the input of Paula, a wind energy expert who he's been in touch with about the next stage of the project.

He sits down at his desk just after 8 a.m. and composes an email to her, explaining his dilemma. He isn't expecting an immediate response as she's based in Salvador, on Brazil's north-east coast. As soon as he hits 'send' on the email he feels lighter. His mind is a bit calmer and he's able to focus on some of the other tasks in his diary.

At around 2.30 p.m. he receives an email from Paula. She offers a number of suggestions, while acknowledging that they all need more work, but at least it's a start. By the time he's driving home he feels better.

****

Coopetition is a term that describes cooperative competition. It occurs on an intra-organisational level and an inter-organisational level.

In the past, traditional corporate companies were in very intense competition for the market. They would be looking for the best way to outsmart their competitors, they wanted the best strategy, the best branding and so on. But the times are changing and we're seeing this especially now with significant global challenges like the Covid-19 pandemic.

Companies are realising that cooperating doesn't have to mean abandoning competition. If we look at the Covid-19 pandemic, one of the biggest challenges is to produce a vaccine. To increase the likelihood of achieving that, companies have to cooperate. But they can still compete in terms of market positioning further along in the process.

At this stage, to develop the product, the smartest thing to do is tap into the brainpower that they have and cooperate with scientists at universities and research institutes. I was delighted to be approached by a biotech company that is working very hard on producing a vaccine for Covid-19 and that needed help with exactly this scenario.

The company is based in Australia, so the first major challenge they faced was that the Australian government stopped all travel into the country. They had to manage this huge project remotely and they contacted me because they wanted to maximise the performance of their virtual teams and reap all the virtual bounties.

The second challenge they faced was in starting the collaboration with their R&D competitors. They decided to cooperate and share their collective brain power to develop the best possible vaccine as soon as possible. But this was a big shift in how they had been working previously, where they were all competing against one another and everything was super confidential.

All of a sudden the scientists had to open their books and share. The barrier they needed to overcome initially was trust. How could they trust each other? How could they really work effectively as a team, disregarding the fact that they ultimately worked for different companies?

In this scenario, another barrier to overcome was that these people are scientists and they really identify themselves with their knowledge and expertise. That means, for some, sharing does not always come as naturally to them as it might in some other professions, such as supply. Sharing isn't their main capital and it requires a lot of trust.

An Evolving Environment

Virtual power teams are an important element of this evolution towards greater coopetition. Virtual power teams were originally born to help teams within an organisation but, as the environment changes, it is evolving to help teams work beyond organisational boundaries.

If you think about the scenario of working with partners and key suppliers, you can see similarities with coopetition. Traditionally, you might have a 100+ page contract between you and your supplier or partner, which has been hashed out with lawyers working on both sides for a couple of months to articulate all the scenarios and service levels and so on.

But often no one refers back to that contract if there is a problem. Instead, people try to balance and resolve it themselves somehow. This is about trust, in this case between you and your supplier or partner, and coopetition is similar. You aim to build trust between human beings, not on a contract-to-contract or lawyer-to-lawyer level, but on a human-to-human, heart-to-heart level.

How to Build Trust

You build trust in the coopetition scenario in exactly the same way that you do when you're building any virtual power team. You use all of the tools and techniques I discussed in Part 1. Get people to present themselves with their lifeline. They should share their journey, the moment they're most proud of, the moment they struggled to discover their natural strengths and talent and so on.

Once you connect in this human to human way, a new feeling emerges. When businesses start to collaborate in this way, the people who suddenly find themselves working together may come with a lot of baggage in that they've been rivals for years. But when you do the exercises I gave you in Part 1, they don't see a competitor they see a human being. This helps them to open up, to collaborate and to see that they can face certain challenges or external issues together. This is about taking the principles of creating a virtual power team and applying them in a bigger context.

The Need for a Collaboration Agenda

Fundamentally, the same principles apply whether you're facilitating intra-organisational or inter-organisational coopetition. Creating the human to human connection by using tools like Personality in Focus and the Strengths Matrix is the starting point and reminds people that we're all human regardless of which company we work for.

The next step is setting that collaboration agenda and this relates to goal setting. You need to set the team goal, which might be something wide like developing a Covid-19 vaccine, but you can introduce other team goals too. These could include how to work more effectively as a team, when you are all coming from different time zones and cultures. Bring this back to your interdependent goals and how you can be most effective as a team.

Structured Communication is Essential

It's vital to have structured communication in all virtual sessions. In the scenario of creating a new vaccine, you might go off in small groups to research, brainstorm and reflect and then come back to a bigger group. That's fine, but when you do come back you need to make sure that you stick with the principles of structured communication that I've discussed in this part of the book.

Everyone should have the opportunity to speak and share something personal about themselves. This reinforces the human connection. When you are sharing ideas, everyone should have a slot to contribute and shine. It's not about just discussing one person's great idea, but about listening to all the ideas. Applying a structure to communication in this community will help ensure everyone is heard.

Finding your Optimal Culture

In Part 3, I'll talk about how to be more effective as a team and how to create your optimal team culture based on all the ethnic cultures involved and using three scales: the leadership scale, the decision-making scale and the conflict scale.

When it comes to coopetition you have to introduce a fourth scale: the sharing scale. At one end you will have the experts who come into a team with their expertise as their main asset and it's one that they're protective of. At the other end of the scale you have the people who are willing to share everything for the greater good.

You have to decide on your optimal position on all of these scales for this particular challenge. Then you have to ask the questions:

- What can I do to support this chosen position? That might require a big stretch to reflect publicly and make that commitment.
- What can the leader do to support this chosen culture, or position, and label it in the best possible way?

I will talk more about these tools in Chapter 10. But this all comes back to what I discussed in the earlier parts of this book, relating to empowering people within teams to build trust, allowing them to choose how they can be most effective as a team, enabling them to choose their goals and milestones based on their strengths, and empowering them to choose their optimal culture.

Don't Forget Personality

I often find that personality is the element that people and businesses forget when creating virtual power teams, both within and across organisations. But there is a very good reason why I put this at the start of my process: because it naturally creates this gravity between team members and, if you unleash people's personalities, it is incredibly powerful.

This is especially the case when you reinforce the ideas from Personality in Focus (Chapter 2) with structured updates. This is further supported with recognition, which I'll discuss in the next chapter, where you can host virtual happy hours, virtual parties and other virtual events to make sure everyone in the team connects and celebrates together.

Defining Intra-Organisational and Inter-Organisational Coopetition

Intra-organisational coopetition: this is between individuals or functional units within the same organisation. In this setting, knowledge sharing between teams is often the primary focus.

Inter-organisational coopetition: this is when two organisations in the same market work together to explore knowledge and research new products while competing for market share. They recognise that working together will lead to greater rewards than working separately, but it requires skill to balance the relationship.

Where Does Inter-Organisational Coopetition Come From?

As I mentioned in my example earlier in this chapter, relating to the Covid-19 vaccine, inter-organisational coopetition often comes from an external force, rather than by choice. But the organisations involved can see that the best way to go forwards is to collaborate, particularly in terms of their R&D.

In a business setting, this will often come down from the CEO, who will see the pressure to create something, but also recognise the potential for exponential growth for everyone if they come up with a completely new product.

In many scientific circles, people may mix with their peers who work for competitors through scientific forums and conferences and so on, but it can be challenging for them to open up and share their expertise in a coopetition environment.

Again, this is where making the human connection is so important, so that they stop seeing one another as competitors and start seeing one another as people, with shared hobbies and passions in life.

Where Does Coopetition Lead?

Coopetition often doesn't end with a project. Once people have discovered one another's natural talents, away from their subject-specific expertise, they reach a new level as a team and they unpack their collaboration further. Often, once a project finishes, this team will be so strong, and have such strong bonds, that they continue collaborating and become a community.

This isn't a new concept. If you look at NGOs, they are part of a wider community and they engage in coopetition all the time. Within the technology sector businesses often behave in a similar way. Concepts such as open-source software and hackathons come from this idea of coopetition.

Coopetition is a much faster way to resolve significant challenges. It allows people to put their heads together, to share expertise and come at problems from different viewpoints to find a solution.

In the past it was often unthinkable because profit dictated everything a business did. Now there is a growing recognition that working together in this way leads to exciting results. Once people start, they continue because solving that first problem creates a marvellous feeling and that's contagious. They see that as a community they're much stronger when they're together and that encourages them to continue working in this way.

Why you Should Explore Cross-Company Coopetition

In our story, we've been following a startup and their journey, which will include some of what I've just talked about in relation to coopetition. But coopetition isn't just a concept that works for startups. It works incredibly well for established corporates too.

There are many reasons to take a coopetive approach:

1. This can help you scale and grow your company much faster.
2. Collaborating with some of your biggest competitors can lead to a revolution in the products that are being developed, while still allowing you to compete for market share.
3. You cannot ignore the environment, the wider world and future generations. You have to be socially and environmentally responsible.
4. You can learn from other industries and sectors that already play on community, such as NGOs and technology. Stay open to seeing how leaders and other industries bring people together to make community work for the greater good as well as corporate profits.

5. Cross-company collaboration and coopetition can help us achieve much greater goals, including some of the toughest challenges humanity has ever faced.

This leads into what I'll talk about in Part 3, where we focus on forming a global community that supports individual business growth as well as helping us work towards solving higher goals that benefit all of us. This next section is about expanding your thinking to a global level and showing you how moving away from being overly internally focused can have benefits for everyone.

High-Profile Examples of Coopetition

Companies around the world are increasingly recognising the need to work together to overcome certain challenges or to develop new and innovative products. The way these companies see it, if they cooperate in a particular field they will have more market opportunities and can then compete in this new spaces in the future.

Here are a few high-profile examples of businesses that have cooperated:

- Samsung and Sony formed an agreement in 2004 to share their research and development costs in a joint effort to design flat-screen LED televisions.
- Apple and Microsoft teamed up to design a mobile operating system.
- Ford and Toyota jointly designed a new hybrid vehicle in 2013.
- Harvard University and MIT formed EDX, a non-profit organisation that provides free online courses, with each of them investing US$30 million.

- Amazon (Kindle) and Apple (iPad) established an agreement in 2007 to allow the distribution of Amazon ebooks through an iPad via the Kindle App. This allowed one party to gain a wider market, while allowing the other to become a more comprehensive content provider.
- Star Alliance Network of competing airlines was established to save on the logistics, marketing and ticketing costs for the airlines involved. The airlines included Air New Zealand, Air China, Thai Airways, United, Lufthansa and Singapore Airlines.

The point is, this is a proven theory that works for many businesses and other organisations across many industries. As you can see, even companies that you would consider big rivals, like Apple and Amazon, sometimes work together if it is for mutual benefit.

How to Establish your Win-Win

Virtual Power Teams Beyond Borders is a method that people from competing organisations, and maybe even different cultures, can use to develop their unique team culture that allows them to make these breakthroughs.

What I'm showing you in this book, through my 10 Big Rocks, is how you can create teams beyond organisational borders; teams that are able not only to improve your business by delivering better results and higher profits, but also to create a better world.

My message, regardless of your focus in terms of R&D, is that if you reach out to the wider community, which could be your competitors as well as your natural partners like universities and research institutes, you could deliver much better results.

However, to deliver these better results you need the people, the experts, on this team, to connect on a human level. They need to have this heart-to-heart connection and then they will build their own nucleus and the gravity that pulls the virtual power team together.

As a leader, this is a daring move. You need to be an empowering leader and not one who micromanages. You have to be part of the decision-making at the right points, and not be the sole decision maker. If you nurture the right environment that allows people to connect on this human-to-human level then one plus one plus one is much more than three on a team level. That also means that one business plus one business equals much more than two in this winning game.

Developing the Right Mindset for Coopetition

Whatever stage your organisation is at in its journey, whether it is a relatively new startup or a multinational corporation with decades of history, you need the right mindset as a leader before you start to leverage coopetition.

Think about our story – how Adam brings in experts like Jeff, Kaito and Sunita initially, but he still needs to learn to provide this nurturing environment before they can run, so to speak. Learning to love and recognise all the strengths within your team is the first stage in learning not to make all the decisions as a leader and to leverage the strengths within your team.

In the next section of the book, you'll find out what happens to Adam and the team when they reach out to R&D partners. They face the same challenges we've already seen, just on a new level, in terms of how open and how committed they are.

I believe that the sooner you are able to forge partnerships like this the better, but (and it's a big but) you must be ready, otherwise you will run into bigger conflicts and potentially not be able to resolve them.

What I mean when I say that you must be ready is that you need to be a team player and a cooperator. Even if you are the boss, you need to be a team player and to respect others, empower others and trust others. It's only once you reach this level in yourself that you will be ready to collaborate on a cross-company level.

PART III

Uniting Global Teams: Leveraging Global Community

9

Praise, Praise, Praise

Paula rolls out of bed and stretches. She walks slowly across her bedroom to the window. She can already tell that it's another sunny day and there's a touch of a breeze, judging by how the curtain is gently flapping at the edges. The heat is already stifling and it's only 7 a.m. She draws the curtain and looks out at the street below. People are out and about already, keen to avoid the worst of the heat in the middle of the day no doubt.

She scrapes her curly hair back into a messy bun and instantly feels a bit better as the breeze catches her neck. She takes a moment, closing her eyes and lets the sun fall on her face before turning back inside and switching the fan on. It hums into life, moving the humid air within her apartment. She's still thinking about the email she received the day before from Adam.

Her initial suggestions were just that, and the more she's thought about it the more she feels there are several workable solutions to the issues he raised. *I guess I can share those in the meeting tomorrow.* She walks into the kitchen and pours herself an orange juice from the fridge. It's cold and refreshing, just what she needs. *Time to get to work!* She knows she needs to prepare before she speaks to Adam and the rest of the team the following day.

****

At 12.50 on Wednesday afternoon, Adam is itching to get started. He's so keen to get on with the meeting and break the news to the team that he logs into Zoom early. He finds himself fidgeting at his desk. Five minutes later, the rest of the team starts arriving. Maya first, shortly followed by Sunita. Then Dave, Jeff and Kaito.

The usual pleasantries exchanged, Adam gets started on the meeting. 'Guys, as you will have seen from the agenda for this week, the first thing we need to discuss is a potential issue with the wind project....' He proceeds to explain the environmental concerns associated with the scheme, specifically its potential impact on migrating birds. 'Ultimately, I think we all agree that what we're trying to do is to the benefit of the planet, and that we don't want to be one of those companies that sacrifices our principles for profit,' he concludes.

Sunita and Maya are both nodding at this. 'Absolutely,' Sunita says. The others are all silent. Adam continues, 'I know this is a lot to take in and I know there will be concerns. I don't have all the answers right now, but I'm sure between us we can work out a plan that will suit everyone.'

This time he sees Kaito and Dave nodding. Jeff is looking stony though. 'Jeff, I get the sense that this is bothering you,' Adam says.

He takes a breath in and says, 'Yes, with the VC that I've raised this change in direction is going to be a serious issue. We could lose the funding Adam.'

There's an awkward silence at this. Adam takes a deep breath and is about to reply when he notices that there's someone in the waiting room of the meeting – Paula. He asked her to join the meeting after 30 minutes to give him a chance to break the news and he was hoping she'd be able to inject some positivity to the situation.

'I appreciate that there are problems we're going to need to solve. I also know that I don't have all the answers, or all the expertise, so I've been working with someone who knows a lot more about wind energy in South America than I do. I've asked her to join us this morning to help us with this, so I hope you don't mind if I let her into the meeting?'

There's a mumbled round of 'Yeah, sure's from the team and Adam brings Paula in. 'Paula, I'd like you to meet the rest of the leadership team here. I know I sort of sprung this meeting on you, but could you just tell the guys a little bit about your background and expertise in the wind energy sector?'

Paula is like a breath of fresh air. She's animated as she talks about past projects, but it's when she starts talking about their current project and the issues that Adam has just raised that her passion really shines through.

While she talks, Adam scans everyone's faces. He can tell Kaito is concentrating. Sunita is starting to smile, and even Jeff is softening. He allows himself a small sigh of relief. Then he realises he needs to concentrate. Paula is talking about the options for reimagining the wind project, one of which is to look at changing the routes and using different sized turbines across the different routes.

'I don't have all the answers to your issues,' Paula says, 'But this would be a logical place to start from my perspective. It would cause least disruption to the scheme itself, it will probably be the most palatable to investors and it solves the issue with the birds. Of course, we'll need to crunch the numbers to be sure.'

She pauses and Kaito jumps in. 'I can help you with the mathematical modelling, Paula.' He launches into a brief overview of his expertise and skills. Sunita is the next to voice her support. Her experience on the R&D of the solar projects could be useful in this respect.

Paula is beaming, they're all starting to talk across one another. Suddenly, Paula pauses. 'I'm so sorry, I have to dash off as I have another meeting across town in half an hour, but can we talk again soon?'

Maya interjects at this point, 'Paula, before you go can you pop your email address in the chat so I can add you to the relevant folders and documents and keep you in the loop? I'm the knowledge manager and collaboration expert, Maya, by the way,' she adds, smiling. 'Sure!' Paula says goodbye, sends her email address and disappears from their screens, breezing out as quickly as she breezed in.

Adam is suddenly aware of the time. They've been on their call for and hour and a half already, which is normally the limit of these meetings. 'I'm conscious of the time, but are you all okay to stay online for another half hour to run through the remaining points on the agenda for today?' he asks.

He finishes the meeting by apologising for the change in direction, adding, 'We don't have all the answers yet, but I'm sure that Kaito, Paula and Sunita will figure it out.'

Jeff has been quiet for much of the call, but Adam sees that he wants to speak. 'Do you have anything to add Jeff?' he asks.

'I'm not sure I like this Adam,' he says. 'I'm sure this Paula knows her stuff, but I'm not convinced we need to be making these big changes to the project. And I can't go to the investors with all this uncertainty. I need hard numbers.'

'I hear you, and I understand your concerns. Kaito, do you think that you and Paula could come up with some revised figures for Jeff by the end of the week?'

'I don't see why not,' Kaito says.

'Great, Jeff, will that help?' Jeff gives a curt nod. 'I can't do anything without firm figures.' Adam can see Maya adding this to the list of action points in their online meeting notes. 'Okay, well unless anyone has anything else, I think we're done for today. Thanks everyone,' Adam says.

Jeff is the first to log out with a brief 'Bye'. Once everyone has left the Zoom meeting, Adam sits back in his chair, interlacing his fingers behind his head. *Well that could have gone worse.*

****

Adam gets up and leaves his office to get lunch and take a brief walk. He's concerned about Jeff. He clearly wasn't happy and he doesn't want him to feel as though he's been left in the lurch. He cuts his lunch break short, only taking half an hour, and returns to the office to call Jeff.

****

By the time Jeff signs out of the Zoom call he can hear the rest of his family stirring. He sits in silence for a while, mulling over what was discussed. *Adam can't just change the business plan on a whim.* He closes his eyes, breathes deeply and centres himself. With each breath he focuses on releasing tension and gradually he feels his anger subsiding. When he feels calm he blinks his eyes open. It's another glorious sunny California day.

He stands up and walks into the kitchen, in search of coffee. Ben hurtles through the door, 'Dad, dad, look at my dinosaur? Isn't it cool?' Jeff laughs, 'Where did you get that?' 'Grammy gave it to me after school yesterday.' 'It's cool. Do you know what kind of dinosaur it is?' Ben barely skips a beat, 'It's an ankylosaurus,' he says knowingly. Jeff smiles again, 'I guess you're the dinosaur expert around here so I'll have to take your word for that!'

Lisa walks into the kitchen as Jeff is pouring a fresh cup of coffee. 'How was the meeting?' Jeff hesitates. 'Not good?' He sighs. 'Just a few issues I wasn't expecting that we're going to have to iron out,' he says. 'Nothing we can't handle.' Lisa smiles. 'Good, pleased to hear it,' Jeff kisses her. 'Back to work I go!' he says, noticing that Ben has positioned his ankylosaurus next to his breakfast bowl. He can't help but smile.

Feeling calmer, Jeff opens his email to see the meeting minutes from Maya. *That woman is efficient!* He opens them and starts reading when his phone rings. It's Adam. *Here we go…*

'Jeff, hi, is now a good time to talk?' Adam asks.

'Sure, thanks for calling,' he answers.

'No problem. Look, I thought it was best if you and I had a chat one-to-one. I'm sorry if you felt blindsided in the meeting this morning, that wasn't my intention. And I know that of all of us, you probably have the most fallout to deal with from this change in direction.'

Jeff begins to nod, then realises that they're on a voice call and Adam can't see him. 'Yeah, I do,' he replies.

'I want you to know that you're not on your own with the investors. I'm happy to fly out to California to face them with you if that's what you need from me, although in the interests of being carbon neutral a video conference might be a better solution. That's your call though, I know that your reputation is on the line with this,' Adam continues, 'Which is why I think it would be good if I could join your next meeting with them, to help explain.' He pauses.

'I appreciate that Adam, thank you. Are you sure that we can trust Paula? Is she really the right person to lean on right now?'

'I've been in contact with her for over a month now since we started exploring this joint venture and she really knows her stuff, as well as the market we're pitching for. And she's not on her own with this, Kaito and Sunita are both supporting,' he says, hoping to placate Jeff and allay at least some of his concerns. 'Do you remember the conversation we had in the early days, where you called me out for not trusting our experts?' Adam asks.

Jeff smiles to himself. 'I do,' he replies.

'I really have learned from that Jeff. It was good advice and now I'm asking that you do the same. At least hold off on judgement until you get the updated figures on Friday....'

'You're right. I have a meeting with the investors next Tuesday, so I'll add you to the meeting and we can do some prep on Monday or over the weekend if we feel we need to,' Jeff says.

'Great. Do you need anything from me in the meantime?' Adam asks.

'No, I think until we get the revised figures on Friday there's not a lot I can do. Thanks for the call Adam.'

They say their goodbyes and hang up. Jeff still feels a little uneasy as he turns back to his laptop, but he does his best to put that to one side and focus on his work.

****

In this chapter we come to the first of the big rocks that makes up my favourite part of the body: the heart. It's actually a rock that I alluded to in the first part of this book. This first rock in the heart is all about recognition and how to recognise progress despite the geographical spread of your team.

Remember that the number one reason why people leave companies is due to a lack of recognition from their direct superior. That means people leave bosses not companies.

I'm the only man in my household. My wife and I have five daughters. If there is one secret that I can share with you that I've learned from being part of a team of six women, it's that you have to praise, praise, praise. The results when you praise someone's behaviour compared to when you don't are very different. I'll tell you for a start that without praise there is no result.

If I see one of the girls helping her sister, I always praise her behaviour. Even if I can't easily see something to praise, I look harder. There is always something you can praise, and in doing so you establish a positive spiral that lifts up the team.

What Qualities do you Need to Stay Motivated When Working Virtually?

To be able to work virtually you need to be a self-starter and self-motivator. You need to be the kind of person who can tackle distractions when they come your way. Once, I was part of a big audience in Bali and we were asked the question: 'What is the number one distraction that kills your motivation when you're working from home?'

The audience voted in real time on their mobile phones, and do you know what the answer was? Netflix. This just goes to show that when you work at home, there are many potential distractions: Netflix, Amazon Prime, social media. You have to be a self-motivator to avoid those distractions.

How to Motivate and Retain Key Team Members When you Work Remotely

But motivation isn't only an issue for individuals. I work with many outsourcing companies, some of which have large remote teams with many of their experts working from home. One of the key issues is how to motivate and retain those experts, because working from home is not always easy.

Do you remember the business I told you about in Chapter 6, whose founders decided to get rid of the office and become digital nomads, only to lose two of their key team members within three months?

One of the reasons for this was that those members of the team didn't have enough motivation, they needed people to interact with in order to feel the joy of working. You have to remember that remote working is not for everyone.

When I work with these outsourcing companies with large home-working teams, we come up with a list of ways to recognise progress. I'll share some of the principles you can use to foster the attitude of gratitude.

Firstly, find reasons to recognise people and celebrate them. When you're giving recognition, there are four things that you need to be:

- Sincere
- Specific
- Selective
- Timely

When it comes to being sincere, I would recommend that you don't start by using words such as 'Great', 'Outstanding' and 'Amazing', otherwise you'll run out of adjectives and superlatives. Instead, start with 'Good', 'Better' and make sure you're able to distinguish the level of performance.

It's also essential that you're honest. Your team members will easily spot when you are praising people just for the sake of praising them. You have to make sure that you feel the person deserves the praise for a particular result or behaviour. But it is important to find things to praise, so if you don't see something at first, look a little harder.

In relation to recognising home workers, I have collected hundreds of working practices and I'll share a few of them with you here.

Photo of the week/weekly highlight: Many people who work remotely are able to work wherever they like. One company I worked with had a space where people could post photos and get immediate feedback, whether that's likes or comments. Whatever it is, the idea is to start a digital interaction and to encourage people to open up as humans, rather than just being seen as 'Experts'. This example allows people to receive instant recognition from their colleagues based on the photos that they share.

My dream office day: This is similar but it actively encourages people to share their working environment. I remember one person posting a photo of their dream office day, which was his laptop on the front of his Land Rover, which was parked at the top of a mountain. That was his ideal office location. As a team, you can decide on a theme for the week, and see what people create. As a manager this is great, because you don't need to do a lot as the rest of the team will recognise each other and generate that positivity.

Create an avatar: This might be a celebrity, or it could be a comic book figure, it can be whatever you like. You'll find that people quickly start joking around and playing around with the avatars. Again, this is about creating meaningful interactions within the team, which fosters that gravity. Someone else's avatar provides another opportunity to have a laugh and integrate local communities if you don't have a single office.

Integrate in local communities: In Chapter 6 I talked about how important it is to help people integrate in their local communities. As a company, I would encourage you to explore how you can support this process. Can you organise some community activities in local co-working spaces? Could you focus on activities with real heart, such as work to make the world a better place, or improve the local environment. Although the idea here is to bring people within a physical community closer together, you should make sure that this is supported by plenty of digital interaction.

Explore how to share: If you have an office, could you use the digital screens in the building to share things like product of the week, or photo of the week? If you don't have a physical office, could you use screensavers for the same purpose? Ask the people on your team to share things. You'll be surprised by how pleased they are to share.

Peer-to-peer recognition: For this you could have an online submission to allow people to nominate others for a particular contribution, such as being a team player. This kind of scheme is easy to set up and you could reward people points for receiving nominations or votes. These points could translate into rewards.

Share the Product of the Week

Encourage peer recognition in the team chat: You don't have to set up an extra tool for this. It can be as simple as saying thank you to someone in the team chat and this will create a positive dynamic. You can make this visual if you want as well. Search for an image that reflects what you'd like to praise and share that. Visual tools are another way to create this culture of recognition and praise.

These are just a selection of ideas to get you to start thinking about how you can easily implement greater recognition within your virtual teams.

As a manager or a team leader it's essential that you're active in this space. Give your likes and comments and you will soon find that participation among your team grows from the early adopters out to everyone as you develop this culture of gratitude and recognition within your whole team.

How to Make Decisions in Hybrid Teams

When I talk about hybrid teams, I mean teams where you have a couple of hubs, maybe head office and some other key locations within your company, but you also have some satellite team members. These are usually people who bring particular expertise to the team that you can't get in your location.

My first tip in this regard is to make sure you provide the full context of a decision to all the team members, because in the hub there are likely to be many conversations happening. People go to lunch together, or they have a coffee break together, but the satellite members of your team are unlikely to have this full context.

Whenever you are making a decision as a team, make sure you share the full context with everyone. The number one skill for leading remote teams is to over-communicate in a positive way.

Share the why, explain the longer term goal and then the particular activity you want the person to contribute to. This is all part of providing the full context.

When I talk about making decisions, sometimes you have several options. There is a wonderful book called *Reinventing Organizations* by Frederick Laloux and one of the examples he shares is of a large community in the healthcare service led by a Dutch entrepreneur. This entrepreneur has a business with

4,000+ nurses who provide health care to elderly people and those who need assistance in their homes.

Before taking any decision, he would write a blog explaining the context and the decision that has to be taken. Then he would list the options without giving his opinion, as well as the pros and cons of each. He would ask people to read the blog and give him their views within 48 hours. Even if not everyone responds, you can start to see what decision the majority would prefer and then the decision is taken.

In the virtual world, there are many opportunities to be democratic and you should take them. As I've said already, micromanagement isn't an option. Before taking a decision, list the options – as a leader be the last one to state your view and encourage everyone to contribute before you share your opinion.

10

Building the Optimal Team Culture

A couple of weeks later, Adam is having his virtual dinner date with Georgia. He sits at the table and sets the tablet up so that he and Rose can both see the screen while they're eating. Of course, for Georgia who is now in California, it's breakfast time.

She's been gone for three weeks and the house feels quiet without her there. But every time they speak, he can tell how much she's enjoying her freedom. Her host family seem like they're taking good care of her.

When Georgia pops up on screen, she is practically bouncing. 'Hi sweetie, how are you?' Rose starts.

'I'm great mum, but dad, there's something I really need to talk to you about,' she babbles.

'Sure, shoot,' Adam says, smiling at Rose.

'The Woodwards, that's the family I'm staying with, took me to this meeting about climate change and some local action that's happening yesterday and I found out about this great group that is working on renewable energy projects in South America,' Georgia barely pauses for breath. 'They're like this NGO and they help businesses just like yours come up with new ideas for renewable energy projects. Isn't that cool?' She doesn't give Adam a chance to answer the question. 'Anyway, I started talking to some of the volunteers and told them about what you do and we all thought it'd be great if you got involved in their virtual hackathon where we could come up with ideas you know, to help you grow and save the planet,' Georgia is beaming and staring intently into the screen.

'Wow, well, I guess I can talk to the rest of the team and see what we can do. I can't promise anything, but it sounds like a great idea to me,' Adam says. He can't help but smile at Georgia's enthusiasm and he feels a wave of pride that she wanted to talk to the NGO about what he did, knowing that if he hadn't changed jobs she'd barely have mentioned him to her new friends.

When they log off the call half an hour later, Adam sits back and beams at Rose. 'She's full of energy isn't she?' Rose eyes him with a smile playing on her lips, 'You're going to get involved in the hackathon, aren't you?'

'I'd like to, I mean I'll need to run it past the team first, but I don't see how it could really hurt…'.

****

Sunita, Kaito and Paula are particularly enthusiastic about the prospect of being part of a virtual hackathon to develop an environmentally friendly app, while Dave, Jeff and Maya also voice their support. Adam is elated. He can just picture Georgia's reaction.

He sets about getting a task ready for the hackathon and, although he wants to see Georgia's reaction on camera, he can't resist sending her a quick text. 'We're in' he types, followed by a big smiley face. Minutes later he gets a response; it's a line of ecstatic emojis. He can't help but laugh.

****

Ahead of the hackathon, Adam has to submit a two-page document outlining what they'd like the team to consider. They know that they want to focus on making gains in the wind sector. After talking with Kaito, Sunita and Paula, he refines the task and sends it to the organisers. *I'm not expecting miracles, but sometimes it can be helpful to get a fresh perspective* he thinks as he presses send on the email. He also has a brief presentation to give on the day of the hackathon, although he feels as though a lot of what he's saying is a rehash of what's in the outline document.

Within a matter of weeks, the hackathon comes around. In spite of himself Adam is excited to see what comes back. He's smiling as he runs through his ten-minute presentation to the teams. *What if they come up with something really great?*

****

Two days later, the results of the hackathon are in. It's 7 p.m. when Adam gets the first email. He's just finished washing up and notices that there are multiple message notifications on his phone. He starts opening them but quickly realises that he'll do better if he opens the attachments on his laptop. He feels excited, almost like a kid at Christmas.

He grabs his laptop from his bag and settles himself in his favourite chair in the living room to start looking at the proposals. There are five in total, from software development teams all over the world, and as Adam opens and reads each he becomes more and more disappointed. Rose, who's curled up on the sofa under a blanket reading a book, notices his changing demeanour.

'What's wrong? Did you get bad news?' she asks, a note of concern in her voice.

'It's these proposals from the hackathon. None of them are any good,' Adam says, placing his laptop on the floor and closing the screen. 'I didn't expect miracles, but none of these ideas are usable for us.'

'What's wrong with them?' Rose asks.

'Well they kind of solve the issue we were exploring, but none of them fit in with our ethos as a company. I have a call booked in with Kaito, Sunita and Paula tomorrow to discuss them, but I don't think any of them are usable,' he slumps back into the chair, looking defeated.

'That's such a shame. Georgia will be so disappointed too. Why do you think they got it so wrong?'

Adam looks up, 'I hadn't thought about talking to Georgia about this! I don't know, I'll talk to the others tomorrow and see if we can unpick it and work out how they went so far off track.'

****

Adam still feels disappointed as he dials into the call the following day with Kaito, Sunita and Paula. Like him, they also feel that the ideas put forward miss the mark.

'I just don't understand why they'd go in this direction,' Adam says.

At this point Maya, who is taking notes in the meeting, looks up from her notepad. 'This might be an obvious question, but did you explain the big picture vision to them along with the task?' she asks.

Adam stops in his tracks. 'I guess I didn't think that would be relevant and I only had a short amount of time to talk to them, so I focused on the specifics.'

Sunita chips in, 'Adam what did you say in your presentation to them? I know we all agreed on the outline document but we never did go over that part with you.'

'Well I just talked about the task a bit more, filled in some of the gaps…' he tails off. It's beginning to dawn on him that he dropped the ball. It's as though no one wants to talk. Paula breaks the silence.

'I know the head of the NGO that organised this quite well. Let me talk to them and see if the groups would be up for another competition. I think if you can share the big picture, the overall vision of what we're trying to do here, you might be quite surprised by the difference in the results,' Paula says.

'Kaito, Sunita, do you think this is worth another try?' Adam asks.

'As long as you don't mind putting in a little more time I don't think it would hurt,' Kaito volunteers. Sunita agrees.

'I think it would help if we facilitated the sessions this time around,' Maya adds. 'I can set up virtual breakout rooms, whiteboards and collaborative spaces so that everyone can get involved.'

'I'd be happy to lead on the sessions,' Paula jumps in. 'I can be on hand during the day to answer questions and steer the groups in the right direction if needed.'

As they sign off the call Adam feels positive but can't help but feel a little sheepish. *Why didn't I consider that?* He sighs and resolves that he'll get the big picture clear in his head in the hope that they can get something out of this the second time around.

****

The next of the big rocks that form part of the heart is establishing an optimal team culture. I'd like to start by telling you about a project that I worked on with a real client that demonstrates how to establish the optimal team culture and shows what you can achieve when you do.

Case Study

The company I worked with was a global, fast-moving consumer goods (FMCG) company that sold baby food. They had a project for €1 billion in revenue with Chinese traders, who were buying their products in ten countries, including Australia, China, Germany, France and Ireland, and putting them on Alibaba.

Because this project was for such a significant volume, the vice president of business development at the FMCG company wanted to accommodate this and get a deal with Alibaba. He spoke to the general managers across those ten countries and asked them to get together, accumulate the volume of goods, and for the Chinese manager to do a deal with Alibaba.

Nothing happened. Of course these were all very busy people and maybe there were some big egos too.

This was when I became involved. I explained the concept of virtual power teams to the vice president of business development at this company and said that I wanted to build the unique culture of this power team.

The vice president of business development decided to create an 18-month project to get this deal with Alibaba. He wanted a solid team, with a clear team vision and optimal team culture. There were 12 people in this team, including someone from HR, the finance director, supply chain manager and PMO. These people were often different nationalities.

Getting Started: Intervention

We started with a one-day workshop in Amsterdam. We chose this approach because their time is very precious and dedicating more than a day to a workshop would have been quite expensive.

During this workshop, we established the team vision and the optimal team culture on three scales, which I'll share with you next.

We explored the team vision from several perspectives, looking at the customer perspective first, and then moving onto the team, purpose and USP perspectives.

The Team's Vision

The team's vision was key to their success. They had a written statement, but they also chose a symbol of success and for this particular team, that symbol was Kung Fu Panda. They chose this character because they felt it embodied the concepts of harmony and agility, as well as commitment.

Source: Peter Ivanov

The Three Scales for Optimal Team Culture

We used three scales to establish this optimal team culture:

- Leadership
- Decision-making
- Conflict

18 months down the road, this project was completed, the FMCG company got its new deal with Alibaba and this generated €80 million profit for the business.

The Leadership Scale

This model is based on one from the book *The Culture Map* by Erin Meyer, but I have simplified it and adjusted it for virtual working when you have a multicultural team.

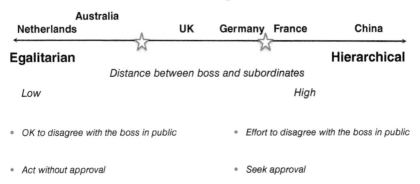

8.1 Leading Scale

On one side of the Leadership Scale you have a hierarchical way of working, and on the other side you have an egalitarian way of working. As you can see from the diagram, some countries tend to fall on one end of the scale, while you'll find others at the opposite end of the scale. This is what Erin Meyer's research discovered.

I've highlighted the key features of the two different ends of the scale below.

Hierarchical

- It takes effort to disagree with the boss
- You have to seek approval
- Meetings with clients/suppliers are conducted boss to boss
- Comms follow the hierarchical line
- You have seating orders with partners

Egalitarian

- It's ok to disagree with the boss in public
- You can act without approval
- Meetings with clients/suppliers are conducted with people at different levels of seniority
- It's ok to communicate with people several levels below or above you
- You have no seating order with partners

In a hierarchical structure, you're not expected to contribute or debate with your bosses and you certainly shouldn't act without getting their approval. By contrast, in an egalitarian structure you're expected to contribute and even to take action without asking for permission.

Within the project for the FMCG company, I asked the senior people in the project team to choose their optimal position on the Leadership Scale. What was interesting was that they actually chose two positions for the different elements of the project.

Their first position was closer to the egalitarian side, which meant they would involve the Chinese partners and work together with them to shape the project mandate.

Once the mandate was determined, they would take a more hierarchical approach to the project. At this stage, they would give the mandate to the Chinese partners now and they would go on to deliver the result.

Distinguishing between these two distinct parts of the project provided a lot of clarity for them. As a group, we reflected on the advantages and disadvantages of choosing these positions. I asked them to consider two additional questions:

1. What can I do to support the chosen position?
2. What can our leader do to support this culture?

It's important to remember, especially when you're working in multicultural virtual teams, that for some people adopting the chosen position might require a significant stretch to behave differently.

What you need to remember is that when you make this process transparent and when the people in the team choose a position themselves and make a team decision, you have an impact on each and every one of them including the leader. As a result, they hold each other peer accountable and a new culture emerges.

Tips For Leaders To Adjust Their Leadership Style

Regardless of where on the scale the team chooses to be, you will still need to lead. Below are some top tips on how to make your leadership style more hierarchical or more egalitarian.

Being A More Hierarchical Leader

- Have a team meeting without the boss to avoid people feeling intimidated
- Give clear instructions on input and participation
- The boss should always chair the meeting
- Invite people to speak up individually in meetings
- Communicate at your level and cc in the boss
- Ask for permission before you address people on different levels
- Use people's surnames unless agreed otherwise

Being a more egalitarian leader

- Manage using performance objectives (instead of short term tasks and micro managing)
- Be a facilitator rather than a supervisor
- Link the objectives to bonuses and rewards
- Regularly check in but allow for self-management
- Dress in the same way as the rest of the team
- Rotate the role of the chairman in meetings
- Communicate directly and avoid cc'ing in the boss

The Four Levels of Meetings

There are four kinds of meetings that you'll have within a team:

- Update meetings: I would advise you to keep these to a minimum and really leverage the use of pre-reads. Make everyone send a one-page pre-read about what they would like to share and limit the meeting itself to sharing key milestones that have been achieved and any obstacles that are in the way. This is the lowest level of collaboration.
- Brainstorming: This is where everybody needs to contribute and not criticise one another. Make sure that everyone knows that they are expected to contribute and that the purpose of the meeting is to brainstorm.
- Decision-making: After you've had a brainstorming session you will need to evaluate the options as a team and make a decision.
- Product development: This is when you co-create or co-design something completely new. Again, you need to be clear on the purpose of the meeting, set the agenda and be clear about what is expected of the participants.

The Decision-Making Scale

In this model, you distinguish between two positions on the scale: top-down, where the leader is expected to decide; and consensual, where you consult all the impacted parties and then make a decision. As with the Leadership Scale, different countries tend to fall in different places on this scale.

8.2 Decision Scale

	Netherlands	Germany	UK	France	China

Consensual   *Decision made by*   **Top Down**

Group   *Individual*

Implementation (no more discussion!)   **Implementation** (more discussion, possible altering of decision)

Debate   **Debate**

Decision   **decision**

I've highlighted the key features of the two sides of the scale below.

Top-down

- Individual decision by the boss
- A short time is spent debating before a decision is made
- The implementation process is longer and may involve further discussion and even lead to the initial decision changing

Consensual

- Group decision by the supervisory or managerial board
- All groups affected are consulted
- A longer time is spent debating before a decision is made
- The implementation process is quicker because there is no further discussion required

When you choose a more consensual approach to decision-making, you create greater transparency and clarity, as well as preempting a lot of the discussions that may happen later on.

Tips for Adjusting Your Decision-Making Process

To move towards the top-down end of the scale:

- Expect the decision to come from the boss
- Be ready to follow that decision, even if everyone wasn't consulted
- Strive to make decisions quickly
- Suggest a vote
- Remain flexible as the decision may change

To move towards the consensual end of the scale:

- Create the meeting agenda in advance
- Expect the decision to take longer
- Demonstrate patience and commitment
- Cultivate informal contacts
- Resist the temptation to make quick decisions

I'd like to make one comment on voting, which can be conducted online very easily using a shared whiteboard that allows people to vote simultaneously for particular options once you've articulated them as a team.

My advice before making a decision is to make sure people contribute, but be wary of going to the far end of the consensual scale, as this may take longer and not be productive. A good middle ground is to articulate the key options, consolidate these and then let people vote. By taking this route, you're still empowering people and taking their views onboard, but you're encouraging a decision to be made.

The Conflict Scale

This scale is about how you disagree with other members of your team. It's important to understand that there are cultures which avoid confrontation. For example, in Asia people are raised from a young age to feel that if they disagree with someone, that person may take it very personally. Therefore they tend to avoid confrontation. In France, by contrast, debating is encouraged in school and you are encouraged to raise confrontational points of view. You need to look at this transparently as a team and decide the optimal position.

8.3 Disagreeing Scale

France	Germany Netherlands		UK	China
Confrontational		☆		**Avoids confrontation**
		Disagreement & debate		
Positive				*Negative*

Here are some of the key features of either end of the scale:

Confrontational

Disconnect the idea from the person sharing it
    Be conscious of connecting the idea to the person
    Be prepared to save face if needed
    Aim to protect harmony within the team
    Prioritise safeguarding relationships

Non-confrontational

Closely connects the idea to the person
Has the desire to save face
Wants to protect harmony within the team
Prioritises safeguarding relationships
Again, as a team it's important to be transparent about how you decide where on this scale you will be.

Tips to Adjust to Different Conflict Styles

- Ask for input in advance
- As the boss, avoid giving your opinion first
- Brainstorm and use tools to allow people to post anonymously
- Have informal pre-meetings one-to-one
- Use the meeting to rubber stamp the decision
- Introduce humour and humility
- Clarify meeting expectations

Finding Your Optimal Team Culture

The most important thing is to choose the culture as a team and then use the tips I've given you under each scale to help you implement that culture and work together effectively.

When you're establishing your optimal team culture, ask the following questions:

1. What is the optimal position for your team on each scale?
2. What are the advantages of the chosen position?
3. What can you do to bridge the gap between the cultures that are distant from your optimal team position?
4. What can the leader do to enable the chosen position?

11

Establishing a Winning Spirit

Two weeks later Adam is preparing to give another presentation to the groups that are part of the NGO and its second hackathon. This time he feels nervous. *What if I don't explain this properly again? What if they don't understand our Why?*

He has worked closely with Sunita, Paula, Kaito, Jeff, Dave and Maya to come up with the 'Why' for the hackathon. It's been a process that has helped all of them reinvigorate their passion for the business, so he feels it has been time well spent regardless of the outcome now.

Adam opens the document Maya has put together based on their meeting. It's a neat list of bullet points with brief prompts underneath. *She's so efficient, how did we manage without her at the start of the company?* He takes a deep breath and composes himself before logging into the virtual meeting where they're ready and waiting for his new brief.

****

The day after Adam has set the task for the second virtual hackathon, he has a much bigger meeting to get ready for. He hasn't even had a chance to check in with Paula about how it all went after he signed out. Along with Jeff, he's meeting with the investors who are, predictably, nervous about the new direction they've chosen to take with their wind project.

Half an hour before the conference with the investors, Adam and Jeff dial into a virtual Zoom call together. Jeff's opinion of the wind project has changed and he's feeling more upbeat, much to Adam's relief. Their chat after that initial meeting where he introduced Paula was tense, but it also cleared the air and Adam was relieved when, the next time he and Jeff spoke one-to-one, they had returned to a much more friendly atmosphere.

I'm glad we can present a united front at this meeting, Adam thinks. The two of them run over some figures and then Jeff tells Adam that he should expect a couple of questions about the company's involvement with the NGO.

'Why?' Adam asks. 'It's not something directly related to their investment.'

'That's true,' Jeff says, 'But you know what investors are like, especially if they get a bit twitchy, they just want to be sure that we're taking care of everything.'

'I think the figures speak for themselves,' Adam replies.

Jeff smiles, 'That they do, but it never hurts to be prepared!'

Adam can't help but smile at this. 'True. Thanks for the head's up.' They sign off the call and each take a quick five minute break to get everything together for the meeting with the investors.

Two hours later, Adam sits at his desk feeling relieved. As Jeff predicted, the investors wanted to know about the NGO and what involvement it had. Adam was thankful for the warning and, thanks to Maya's organisation, he was able to pull up the figures and details they needed within minutes.

But as he and Jeff discussed, the figures speak for themselves and Adam is confident that, even if nothing comes from their partnership with the NGO in an R&D sense, the company has a solid base across their existing solar projects to carry them through.

The wind project is also taking shape and has come on a long way since Paula became involved. He allows himself a minute to close his eyes and breathe. *What a week! And we still have the second round of proposals from the NGO to come yet.* He glances at his inbox. Although that has thankfully got quieter in recent months, there is still plenty for him to deal with. He stands to go and get a cup of coffee before he starts to tackle the emails though.

****

It's not until Friday afternoon that the new proposals from the NGO hackathon start rolling in. Adam is excited and nervous at the same time. He almost can't bring himself to open them. One by one, the app prototypes spring into life on his desktop. He starts to explore them. By the time he's partway through the third of five proposals, he's grinning. These seem like much more suitable suggestions. He glances at his inbox to see that Paula is requesting a meeting with the leadership team on Monday. As he opens the meeting invite, he sees a short note she's added: 'Sorry, too excited to wait until Weds to go through these proposals!' He grins. Monday it is.

****

The weekend has given them all time to play with the apps and to read and digest the accompanying proposals. There are two particularly strong candidates as far as Adam is concerned. As they all log into Zoom, the mood is very different to the previous session, when there was an air of disappointment. When Paula dials in, a wave of excited energy seems to flow out of the screen.

She's particularly expressive with her arms and hands today and the rest of them can see how excited she is. By the end of the hour, they have settled on two of the proposals, one that relates to wind and one that relates to solar.

Paula is almost bursting with excitement. 'I would love to lead on the wind energy proposal. I have some great ideas about how to bring this forward and with some of the other people in my network out here I think we can make real headway.' She gets no objections from the rest of the team.

Kaito and Sunita agree to take a joint lead on the solar proposal. Until this point in the meeting Jeff has been quiet and Adam is worried that he's not happy about the direction they're taking. He steals a glance at Jeff in the corner of his screen and notices that he's smiling.

As the babble of discussion surrounding the proposals dies down, Adam asks, 'Jeff, is there anything you'd like to add?'

'Sorry, I've been a bit quiet, haven't I? Just taking it all in. As a matter of fact I was just thinking about what Paula was saying and I'm confident I could find us some financial backers for a project like that, provided we make some progress in the coming weeks.'

Adam's face lights up. 'Brilliant.' He's not sure what he's more happy about: Jeff's assertion that he can probably source additional finance or the fact that he seems fully onboard with the project.

After everyone has left the meeting, Adam, once again, finds himself sitting at his desk letting the meeting sink in. It's becoming a habit, taking this minute with his eyes closed to mull over what's been said. As he opens his eyes, he sees Dave standing at the door to his office.

'What's up Dave, you need me for something?'

'All good. I just wanted to pop by and say well done with the second round of proposals from the NGO. I think we've got some really solid ideas and this could take the company to the next level. I'm popping out for a coffee, you want anything?' Dave smiles.

'I think I'm okay for now, but thanks. And Dave, thank you for all your support with this.' Adam watches him walk away and takes a deep breath. *Who would have thought this is where we'd be ten months ago?* He shakes his head, clears his mind and focuses on his computer once again.

****

Establishing a winning spirit within your team is the ninth big rock and I'd like to begin this chapter by telling you a story about how you can inspire this winning spirit, even when you're physically distant from your team.

In 2006/07 I was a project manager for a project to establish new global IT shared services. This was part of a global program and I was responsible for 20 countries in Europe. The goal was to transfer the IT services management from local IT management in those 20 countries, with local people and local suppliers, to the global shared centre that was based in Kuala Lumpur, Malaysia.

My Team[1]

Initially I had two people on the team, a German lady called Inge and an Uzbek man called Makhmud. Inge spoke five languages and was super organised; she was the ideal PMO. Makhmud was a larger than life individual who lived in Moscow.

The three of us were supported by five global experts in HR, legal and tax. The HR expertise was necessary because the project involved restructuring the business, so people would get a new job description and a new boss. The legal expertise was important because of the new contract and new service level agreements with the new legal entity. And the tax expertise was important because the recharging mechanism and invoice came from a different international legal entity.

The Early Stages of the Project

At the start of the project there was a lot of enthusiasm among the team members. It was fun for everybody and we were all part of a business trip to Kuala Lumpur because this project was high on the radar of the global corporation that I was working for at the time.

But three months in, I noticed that the feeling in the team had changed. I noticed that I was often trying to be the 'smartest person' in the room. Not only was I telling everyone what had to be done, but I was also telling them exactly how it should be done. I'd like to add that looking back I believe that deciding what we had to do should have been a team effort.

---

[1]Names have been changed

What I observed was that, in the meetings where I was trying to be the smartest person in the room, this didn't go down well with the experts who were part of this team. I noticed that after such meetings, it was neither possible for me to push nor motivate my team members. At this point I realised that, instead of being a productivity factor, I had become a break factor with the fallout just waiting around the corner. I had to do things a different way.

Taking a Different Approach

While I was contemplating this, Makhmud left the team because he had organised a career move for himself. Lucia, a Spanish lady with a red mane of hair and a slightly husky voice, replaced him. She brought the fresh wind of change that we needed.

Lucia suggested that we all complete the lifeline exercise, which I told you about at the beginning of the book. By this stage there were five of us working full-time on the European project: me, Inge, Lucia, Eric and Steve.

When everybody presented their lifelines I was amazed. I had been stupid enough to compete with these people and all of a sudden I realised how lucky I was to have the chance to work with such talented people.

After this exercise, for the first time, we took a bottom-up approach. It wasn't me telling everyone what to do and it was a team effort on the goal. The process wasn't as streamlined then as it is now, with the interdependent goals and roadmaps, but it made all the difference.

Six months down the road, we had gathered so much momentum as a team that I went to the project board and suggested that if we finished this two-year project three months early, the company should pay for all 30 people who were involved – the five members of the European team, five global experts and 20 IT transition managers located in each country – to go away for two days to Tenerife in the Canary Islands.

Europe was by far the most complex region for this restructure. As you may well know, carrying out a restructure and reorganisation in countries like Germany and France can be a bit of a nightmare, so the target was certainly a stretch. The project board agreed to send all 30 of us to Tenerife if we completed three months early.

If you're wondering why, the reason is simple: money. The people cost of this project was €1 million per year. There were ten of us managing this project full time: five in Europe and five global experts. If we finished this project three months early, we would save the company €250,000.

I immediately announced this to the team and the spirit was completely different, particularly among people from places such as Belarus or Uzbekistan, who might find it difficult to afford this kind of trip themselves.

The Road to Tenerife

Inge came up with a creative way of reporting our progress, and it looked something like this.

9. WINNING SPIRIT

The island is obviously Tenerife and each of the 20 parachuters represented the IT transition managers in each country and we had lines to mark milestone after milestone. Prior to this we had been using more standard traffic light reporting, but all of a sudden we now had a very visual and engaging way to chart our progress. Everyone can see at a glance where we were with the project.

Initially, the competition was about which parachuters would land earliest on the island, but after the first few had landed this became irrelevant because we would only deliver if we all made it, otherwise nobody would get to go.

Week after week and day after day as we approached the deadline the suspense was rising. You could see at a glance who was available to help and who needed help. This created a wonderful spirit of cooperation.

Just one day before the deadline, on 30 December 2007, the last parachuter from Uzbekistan landed on the island.

The Outcome

At the end of this project, we received great customer feedback, so working quicker wasn't at the expense of quality. We saved €200,000 net. Then we had a fantastic party.

How to Apply This to Your Team

What are the morals of this story that you can apply to your team?

1. *Be generous*
   Firstly, if you set a prize for outstanding performance then be generous. Remember that you can afford to be generous because the organisational cost of a delay is much higher. If you increase productivity significantly and you save a lot of money then you can find the funds for a generous prize. If you just set an average prize, people won't have enough of an incentive. So that is the first moral: be generous.

2. *Give people time*

   The second moral is to announce it early enough that your team has a chance of achieving it. You need to give a large virtual team at least six months to tune into the prize and see how cool it would be if they could all celebrate together.

3. *Make it a team experience*

   The third moral is to make it a team experience. The reason for choosing a team experience and not money is that money devalues very quickly. It should also be a team experience that is chosen by the team to have maximum impact.

4. *Chart progress visually*

   Finally, it's very important for virtual teams like this that you have a visual way of charting progress. Obviously, in the example I just shared we used parachuters, but I've worked with numerous clients who all came up with different, creative and beautiful visual representations of a project.

   Being visual is really important because it allows people to see where the team is at a glance. Make sure it's updated daily so that those who are able to can offer help to those who need it.

What if You Don't Have the Budget to Be Generous?

I have been lucky enough to work with several NGOs who have zero budget to offer generous prizes, but in this instance you need to think creatively. For example, I work with an NGO called Youth Against AIDS here in Germany, which is a large organisation; but there are only six people on the management board who don't take a salary and there are 6,000 volunteers across Germany. This means they don't have a budget for the kind of prize I got for my team when I worked for a big corporate organisation.

But Youth Against AIDS do have sponsors, so they managed to agree a prize with one of their sponsors. In this case, it was tickets to a Bayern Munich game. You can imagine how this helped motivate people to go the extra mile, so they got the results they wanted from a project and their team got the football tickets.

I also work with the Bulgarian branch of the American NGO Teach For All, who found a simple way to say thank you to their volunteers. They had a virtual pizza night. It was very simple, they got all 150 volunteers to order the same meal – a pizza – with similar drinks and then they all put the same music on and had a virtual party in their location.

This demonstrates what you can do with a bit of creativity, even if you don't have a big budget. Just make sure that your team knows what constitutes outstanding performance and let them choose the prize.

Use Tangible Tokens

As well as working out what prize will act as a magnet for your team, it's good to think about whether you can introduce tangible tokens.

In today's world, many things are online and digital and sometimes it's good to have tangible tokens.

For example, when I was working in IT services across Eastern Europe, the Middle East and Africa, we used to have a Champion of the Month. This is related to recognition, and the way it worked was that people within the team would nominate somebody online who had made the biggest contribution in terms of supporting achievements.

When the Champion of the Month was chosen, we used to ship them a beautiful African doll that they could put on their desk. When people asked about it, the champion could explain what it was and why they had received it. Each month this doll would pass on to the next champion.

Don't Forget About People's Families

Also remember that in virtual teams very often the families also suffer because they are impacted by the fact that this person works in a global team. That sometimes means you have to take part in online meetings very early or very late in the day. In the Middle East you might have to join a meeting on a Friday, which is the weekend for them.

What I used to do sometimes when the results were great was send vouchers for a dinner for two to each team member, so that they could take their partner out for a meal. The idea was that, at least once a year, they would feel recognition from the company for their work.

These are just some suggestions, but there is a whole host of ideas for how to celebrate your team and their achievements.

12

Next Generation Leaders

A month later, the projects have really accelerated, especially the wind project. He's just finished a call with Paula and they need to get their new turbines in production before Christmas if they're going to meet the project deadlines. It's a tall order. Adam has already put out feelers for a manufacturer, but the most logical option is to go with their existing partner in China.

He has a good relationship with them and he decides to email the production manager to set the ball rolling. To his amazement, they agree to deliver the first of the new turbines within two months of starting production. Adam does a quick calculation, that would put them in January, which is tight but doable. He's excited and relieved. He sends a quick email to Maya, asking her to add this to the agenda for their team meeting the following week.

****

Adam wakes early as usual, feeling as though he's slept well. Getting the process of manufacturing the wind turbines started was a weight lifted yesterday. He picks up his phone as he sits up in bed and sees a WhatsApp message from Kaito. *That's unusual.* Suddenly feeling a knot form in his stomach, he opens it.

'Adam, we have a problem. You need to check your emails and call me as soon as you get this okay? It's about the wind turbine production.' Hurriedly, Adam opens the emails on his phone. It doesn't take him long to find the email Kaito is referring to. It's from the president of the company politely informing him that they have other priorities and won't be able to deliver the turbines to the schedule that was agreed. Instead the first turbines won't be ready until late spring.

Forgetting that Rose is still asleep, Adam slams his hand down on the bed in frustration. Rose jumps, 'Adam, what are you doing?' 'I'm so sorry Rose, just a work issue I need to sort out, you go back to sleep.'

He pulls on a jumper and goes downstairs. He's reeling from the email. *Why would their production capability change so dramatically, and so quickly?* He can't fathom it. While the kettle is boiling he realises he needs to call Kaito.

He makes a coffee, composes himself and then goes to his home office. Kaito answers almost immediately. 'Did you read the email?' he asks, barely saying hello.

'Yes and I don't understand. I agreed everything with them yesterday, this doesn't make any sense.'

'Who did you agree this with Adam?' Kaito asks.

'The production manager. I forget his name off the top of my head, but we've been dealing with him since we started working with them,' Adam explains.

'Ahh,' Kaito says. 'Now this makes complete sense.' Adam can't tell if he's missing something obvious because he's not fully awake yet.

'It does?' he asks.

Kaito half smiles. 'Sorry, but it does. You see, in Chinese culture it's considered highly disrespectful to agree anything like this with someone who's considered a junior member of staff. You need to get permission from the senior managers before you start dealing with the production manager, especially for a large-scale order like this.'

Adam listens and processes the information. It hadn't occurred to him at all. He'd been so excited to get the project moving, and feeling pressure from the investors, as well as Paula and the project team to push things forward. He lets out a sigh. 'Can I fix this?'

'You can try. The best thing to do right now is to show respect to the president and apologise for the way you went about things. If he accepts your apology, you might be able to renegotiate the delivery dates with him,' Kaito suggests.

'Okay. Kaito, could you see if you can organise a meeting with him for me? I feel as though you might be better placed to do that than I am at the moment. I'll fill Jeff in today as I think he should be part of this meeting too as it could have financial implications for us,' Adam says.

Kaito agrees. 'Adam, don't be too hard on yourself. This isn't ideal, but we should be able to sort it.'

'Thanks, I hope you're right.'

The following day they have a meeting with the president of the manufacturing company. Kaito has helped Adam find the best way to word his apology, for which he is incredibly grateful. With Jeff's assistance, they've also calculated how much more they can afford to pay to hit the delivery dates they need. Adam feels a little nervous, but is quietly confident he can pull this off.

After apologising and much negotiating, the president of the manufacturing firm agrees to some slightly revised production deadlines, but nothing that will throw the project out by too much. However, it will cost Adam nearly double for the turbine order now. That's within the range he agreed with Jeff and he's mostly relieved that he's been able to solve the issue with minimal disruption to the project timeline.

Jeff is stoic about the situation. 'That's how it goes sometimes. Not ideal but it could have been worse,' he tells Adam with a wry smile. Kaito believes the apology helped with the negotiations. As they sign off the call Adam suddenly feels exhausted. He didn't sleep well last night and now the stress has gone he can feel his energy levels dropping. *I'm taking the afternoon off.* He sends a couple of quick emails, sets his 'out of office' and then heads for home.

****

Autumn has turned to winter. Adam's early morning gym sessions feel like more of a struggle in the darkness, but he knows that once he's there and pumping weights he feels on top of the world. The one good thing about moving into December is that Georgia will be home for a visit at Christmas. Both he and Rose have been finding it challenging to be apart from her for so long.

Glancing at the clock on the wall of the gym Adam realises that he needs to hurry. Jeff has called an impromptu management meeting for that afternoon and he has a lot he wants to do before the call. It's to discuss the prospect of the company making an Initial Crypto Offering (ICO) and Adam wants to make sure he understands all that this entails before they start discussing their options.

There's a buzz on the call. Jeff is visibly excited. He leads the meeting, explaining what an ICO is, what it will mean for the company and why they need to do it now. 'My research suggests that a rival energy company is going to come out with an ICO soon. We've done so much work to get ahead in this space and I'd hate to see us lose out because we weren't quick enough off the mark,' he explains.

'When would we need to make the ICO by?' Kaito asks.

'End of January,' Jeff responds. There seems to be a collective intake of breath.

'That doesn't feel like very long, especially with Christmas coming up,' Dave says.

'I know, it's fast, but we don't want to miss this opportunity and allow someone else to come into this space and disrupt before us. I'm not exaggerating when I say that we're at the forefront here,' Jeff enthuses.

There's more discussion, and questions about how it could affect the ongoing solar and wind projects. Adam has been listening. He can sense there's some reluctance among the team, but he's also convinced it's just because it's such a big step, not because they don't believe in themselves. He decides it's time to say his piece.

'I know it's a lot to take in and it is undoubtedly a big step for us,' Adam begins. 'But look at how far we've come and all that we've achieved in a year. This is going to be a lot of work and yes, like Jeff says, the timing is tight, but I believe in all of you and what you're capable of. I know we can pull this off. It really will catapult us forward and help us do even more good in the world.' He pauses. Jeff is grinning. Sunita and Paula look more relaxed. Kaito is harder to read, but Adam senses a smile playing on his lips. Dave and Maya are both nodding.

'It's incredible that we've done so much given that we've never all met one another,' Maya says, as though thinking out loud.

Adam agrees, 'It is incredible, and that's why I know we can do this too. What do you say? We all need to be in agreement to go ahead with this. . .'

One by one they agree. 'Let's do this!' says Jeff, clapping his hands together. There's a palpable excitement among the group, even though they're spread across continents.

'I have an idea,' Maya says. 'Why don't we say that if we pull this off and meet this deadline, that we all meet somewhere for the first time.'

Adam's face lights up. 'That's a great idea Maya and I know the perfect place… Brazil.'

Paula looks dumbfounded, 'What? You'll all come here?' Adam thinks it's the first time he's ever seen her lost for words. He laughs.

'Why are you laughing?' Paula asks with a grin. 'I think it's the first time I've ever seen you speechless!' Adam replies, to a round of laughter from the rest of the team. Paula positively cackles.

'But where better to meet than the test location for our wind turbines?' Adam says with a grin. Now they're all really excited.

At home that evening he tells Rose what they've decided. 'That's incredible. And you're sure you can meet that deadline?'

'When we're working together like this I think we can do anything we put our minds to,' Adam says, hugging her warmly.

****

Next generation leaders is the tenth and final big rock that you need to build your virtual power team and I'll tell you why it's such an important one.

You can have the best virtual power team on top, where you're applying all nine of the big rocks that I've already talked about, but this won't be of much value if you have ivory tower syndrome, where your senior leadership team is very aligned but there's a disconnect between this team and the other layers of the organisation.

It's essential that you involve other organisational layers to deliver your agenda and this is where developing next generation leaders is vital. Many multinationals have a global HR function, which means they usually have a way of categorising leadership talents, by which I mean they identify the people who have the talent and appetite to lead.

This group can have different names – it might be potential leaders, high potential – but whatever it is, it's important for you to use the work done by the HR team in the career development sessions to find those next generation leaders.

If you don't have this HR structure in your organisation, then it's important that you as a team look to your extended teams and nominate the people who have the potential, skills and appetite to become next generation leaders.

Once you have identified these people, however you do it, you need to involve them in delivering the roadmaps. This is where demand meets supply. Your leaders cannot deliver their interdependent goals based on the roadmaps without the support of people in the organisational layers below them, as well as people in different locations, to deliver this agenda.

Building Virtual Power Teams Under Virtual Power Teams

What you need to do is get each of the leaders within your virtual power team to identify three to five people with leadership talents within their direct reports. These people then form a new virtual power team and you get them to work on the three roadmaps you identified to work on the biggest opportunities or challenges you face.

You're creating virtual power teams at different levels of your organisation and this supports everyone as you move higher up the chain.

This is not only the best way to deliver your strategic agenda, but it's also the best way to develop new talent within your team and create your next generation leaders by allowing them to get involved on real strategic projects.

Ways to Develop Next Generation Leaders

Getting them involved in strategic projects is just one part of the puzzle. You can also bring them into certain elements of your structured communication. Remember that I talked about having a formal monthly meeting, where each team member talks about where they are at with their strategic goal? Use these meetings to introduce your next generation leaders to this level of management.

Inviting your next generation leaders to join one of these meetings and present to the senior leadership team provides a significant motivational boost. Allowing them to be part of that team, to answer questions and to get exposure to senior leaders is not only one of the best ways to deliver on your strategic goals, but also to develop the leaders of the future.

Top Tips

- Avoid ivory towers
- Develop leadership talents
- Engage and involve everyone with the strategic agenda

Case Study

I'm going to tell you a story now to illustrate how important next generation leaders are to the success of your projects. This is a project I led in 2012. We even won an award called Global IT Connect, which we were given for this project called Wide Area Network, More for Less. At this time, I was head of IT services in Eastern Europe, the Middle East and Africa at my organisation.

Source: Peter Ivanov

Our biggest challenge was poor infrastructure and poor network connections in some places, particularly in Africa and countries in central Asia like Uzbekistan. Half of our budget, a multi-million dollar figure, was dedicated to the Wide Area Data Network. That meant we were paying a fortune and still not getting a good service. We needed to tackle this challenge.

Assembling the Team

I'm not strictly technical, so instead of me figuring it out, we had a session as a team where we discussed the priorities and this was identified as one of the strategic goals. One guy called Olakunle from Nigeria got the goal and we picked people from all the critical locations with leadership talent, as well as people from other locations, to help him work it out.

The team was made up of both junior level managers and experts and they had complete freedom over decision-making.

The Outcome

After nine months, I think we got five times more bandwidth for half of the cost. This was amazing. But achieving this didn't actually solve the biggest problem.

The biggest problem was that this team designed it using something called IPSec to use the internet and deliver a secure connection that was much better than what we received from our current global provider. The challenge came from engaging with the organisation and we encountered a lot of internal resistance.

But with my political support the team carried on and we mobilised other senior people within the region who were suffering as a result of this poor connection, who were also paying money to receive a substandard service. Eventually, we managed to crack this internal organisational resistance and that was what led to the team receiving the award.

The CIO of the organisation presented the award and all the key team members were there. The CIO said that what the team achieved was amazing, in terms of securing five times the bandwidth for half the price, but that the biggest achievement was our persistence, perseverance and determination not to give up in the face of organisational resistance and bureaucracy.

Why Did We Persevere?

There are several reasons why some people persevere and don't give up, while others are defeated by bureaucracy. The first is clear ownership. The second is that you have to be doing something that is meaningful for the team, something that really matters. The third is giving constant encouragement that they are on the right track.

This is important in big corporations especially, because teams like this need help. In this scenario, no matter how brilliant you are technically, if you don't have the political support to engage at different levels of the organisation then you don't succeed.

My role within the team was to give them this political support, to engage and get some other people to support what we were doing.

Bringing a Fresh Perspective

I also remember another Nigerian team member Nwankwo who asked the CIO a difficult strategic question. It wasn't a question that the seasoned managers were asking. The CIO congratulated him, first of all for being bold enough to speak up and ask, but also for asking a valid question.

Next generation leaders often come with a completely different perspective and it's a matter of integrating them, putting them to work on the strategic agenda, but also making sure that they are heard. You need to allow space for them to challenge you and you then need to act on the promises you make.

Key Takeaways

This reinforces the importance of next generation leaders in relation to the other things I've discussed. So you set the nucleus as a team, you decide on the big priorities and then you allocate people who have a passion as well as the skills to work on this goal. You have to give them full decision-making freedom. Look at what happened in my team; they thought outside the box by going towards an internet-based protocol, which elsewhere in the organisation would have been unthinkable because we had a global supplier, and so on. You also have to give them a lot of support. You need to give recognition and praise, but remember they may also need physical support to align some of the stakeholders with what they're doing or to get approval.

Virtual Power Family

I'd like to introduce you to the concept of the virtual power family. Like the virtual power team, the virtual power family has a very clear vision and goal or goals. This vision and goal is the nucleus of the atom, and then you have the particles flying around. The only way to prevent the particles, which are the people in your team or family, from getting lost in space is to make sure they are attracted to the nucleus. That's why the nucleus needs to be the mission and vision for the family.

In a virtual power family, you need to find this core nucleus when your family members start to go in different directions and are not all in the same place to make sure they are still attracted and that you still have this strong gravity.

You can apply many of the principles of a virtual power team to a virtual power family. Everyone needs to work on their strengths and work as a team, not just to do the necessary housekeeping, but also to celebrate success, birthdays or other occasions.

As well as having their goal, they're aware of each other's strengths and they'll ask for help when they need it. This is sometimes forgotten in families, but it's one of the elements that's really applicable from virtual power teams. So uncovering everyone's strengths and talents, and making sure these are explicitly known by all family members.

When we uncover our strengths as a team, we make avatars with celebrities or movie characters, and you could do something similar within your family, so that you are all really working to your strengths and helping each other. This is really important as people start to move away, so you need to establish rituals in your virtual family to keep the gravity despite the distance. In my family, we set our family goals, mission and vision on a regular basis.

Why it's Important to Foster Gravity in Your Virtual Family

Establishing these rituals and keeping this balance is really important in a virtual family because they really make a difference to your connection when you aren't physically in the same place. If you don't establish these kinds of rituals, you can miss opportunities.

If everyone is just focused on themselves and their vision, with no rituals that highlight opportunities and no drive to cooperate, people can become more distant, almost as if they are closing themselves off in a cocoon. Even though you love the people within your family, there is a higher chance of them getting on somebody else's nerves.

I think by learning from each other, and this has to be ritualised, by helping each other and by having a clear focus based around your strengths, you change your focus as a family to positive things. You are inspired by the goal and vision that you set, and that helps you to tackle things that other families might struggle with.

I also believe that this approach helps you get more joy, because you are more focused and aligned as a family. You are all able to achieve more because when you're working towards a common goal with the people that you love you'll stretch yourself more and probably develop more to get there.

What Can You Learn From Being Part of A Virtual Power Family?

It's safe to say that in a family the care elements will be better established than they are in a business organisation. But the more care you can bring to the business environment, the better. This may sound too altruistic, which is why I link it to the goals set by the team and the big 'Why' that explains the reasons we do everything.

Then you bring in the strengths and, as I mentioned in the first part of the book, you need to do the lifelines exercise to show the uniqueness of each individual team member. You have to take time to explore this, to recognise their uniqueness and to drill down to see what their unique strengths and talents are. When you do this, people start to care more in a business context.

Using the principles from this book will therefore bring you success in your family, as well as in your business.

Applying These Principles to Long-Distance Relationships

You can also apply the principles from virtual power teams and families to long-distance relationships. I'll share some tips that I picked up from a friend of mine who is also a speaker and an actress called Tara. She doesn't have kids but her partner does, and they now live in a long-distance relationship. These are her top tips to make this work:

Have One Channel of Communication

WhatsApp is an app that most people know and it's a good choice because you can leave voice messages even if you are in different time zones, which can bring a more personal touch to your communication. It's better than texting because people can hear the melody and tone of your voice.

A couple of times a day, leave your partner a voice message and it makes a difference if this is coming from the heart.

Send Pictures

If you're in a different location, take a picture, put a comment or emoji alongside it and maybe leave a voice message. We all do this, but the important thing here is to do it more consciously. Do it more regularly. This will help you sustain relationships.

Be conscious in your communication and communicate regularly and you will see a difference.

Maintaining Global Friendships

These tips don't only apply to romantic relationships, they are also applicable as you develop friends as an individual. The more global the lifestyle you lead, the more likely it is that you'll have friends in different locations.

You have to maintain the relationship in the virtual on a regular basis. This isn't a silver bullet: get in touch once a month or whatever makes sense – the key is that it's regular. One of the advantages to having friends in different places is that you can decide to meet up in an exotic location. This may require you to have a more entrepreneurial lifestyle where you have more freedom but, if you can, arrange to meet someone in a specific location and catch up properly for a week and enjoy life together,

Having a global lifestyle brings more opportunities to see friends with a mix of the virtual and the physical. If you can make your physical get-together somewhere exotic then even better.

If you stay with friends when you travel, you could ask if you could walk their dog, or read a story to their child – just something to bring a more personal touch. This can be a nice way to travel, especially if you don't yet have your own family and home base. It allows you to experience the emotion and support of a family while you're a global citizen.

It's also important to protect your free time, and particularly your weekends, to physically meet people and spend time together. If you work with someone during the week, it's important to have that time outside of work to really create a deep connection.

Connect With Your Parents

Some people may not have kids and a family of their own, but they will more than likely have parents. If you live a virtual lifestyle, maybe as a digital nomad, and you're in a different location to your ageing parents, it's quite common to feel guilty that you're so far away.

One of my top tips is to have a daily happy hour with your parents via a video call. You can have a standard agenda and just talk about your highlights of the day. Even just calling it the virtual happy hour puts a positive spin on it – remember Adam having his virtual happy hour with his daughter Georgia in our story?

Even if you're away or living in another country, that doesn't mean you have to be emotionally distant. With technology, you can still be together.

Co-living to Be Part of A Community

There are many cities around the world where co-living is common, particularly among younger people. There are some ways in which you can make the most of this arrangement to become part of a community of like-minded people.

When you're looking for somewhere to live, or for a new housemate, you could do some preselection filtering. Find out if you have common interests or a common mission and look at how you can help each other, maybe in terms of networking, referrals or just having idea generating sessions.

There are several advantages to co-living, especially if you are moving to a new place every year or so for work.

The first is that it allows you to feel as though you're part of a family. Even though the people you move in with will be strangers at the beginning, they often become close friends and you connect in a similar way to a family. But you still have a balance between that community and your own privacy, because you are living in your own room.

The second is that your communication skills will improve. Having to manage a living space with people you don't really know can be a challenge, but it will teach you a lot about how to handle different personalities and maybe how to have slightly difficult conversations. There are also other elements that we've discussed in relation to global power teams, in terms of dividing up activities and everyone being responsible for their own goals or tasks.

The final advantage to mention here is that it can be fun and introduce you to people you would never otherwise meet. It's a learning experience.

The Importance of Community

I talked earlier in the book of helping your remote teams to become part of their local community, but this is a very important point, especially in the world we now live in. There are some companies with over 1,000 employees without a single office and everyone working remotely.

One of the challenges they have when everyone lives and works remotely is that sometimes their emotional needs are not met. They need to be part of a community and that's why it's important for companies to invest in co-working spaces and to even look at how they can sponsor some of the local communities people want to join so that they can create this balance and this family feeling.

The more virtual we become, and the more remote we become, the more important it is that we create that local community connection.

My Advice for Living and Working Remotely

If you are working virtually and living alone, and you are one of these particles orbiting the nucleus, know that you are never actually alone. Whatever city you happen to live in, there are things you can do.

One of them is to make sure you stick to your regular happy hour with your mum or dad.

Another is to follow the never-eat-alone principle. What you do is send a message to all your contacts who live in that city. They might be other people from the business you work for, or people you have met elsewhere. But use the technology to send a message to people who are in your location and ask if they are around and if they would like to go for drinks or dinner. We all have to eat, and this can be a good opportunity to meet people if you are somewhere alone.

I've certainly experienced brilliant ideas being born out of such catch-up lunches. For example, I have a friend who was a part of a Bulgarian startup that had created an app around Food waste reduction. They connect restaurants that have leftover food with the people who might need it. The app was up and running, but needed a bit of a push to really gain momentum. I put the people involved in this startup in touch with a friend of mine who is an ambassador for the UN Sustainable Development Goals around hunger. This contact opened up a lot of potential for the startup and their app. All of this was born out of a catch-up lunch. We didn't have this agenda in mind. So, my top tip is to never eat alone, you never know, you could end up changing the world.

You should also think carefully about how you behave when you're on work meetings or calls and make sure that you know whether people can see you as well as hear you. Implement Consulting Group has carried out research which found that 47% of people have gone to the bathroom during a virtual meeting. Of course, if you have your video on and don't realise it, this could go very badly!

Setting Up Your Virtual Working Environment

It's important to be able to mentally separate your work and home environment when you work remotely. I would also say that if you're working from home, you want to be doing work that you love and that aligns with your values, otherwise it can be difficult for your mental health if you feel as though you can never escape from it.

I have some practical tips for setting up a home office and separating your work and home lives:

1. Create a work zone. This needs to be a space where you are comfortable working and are able to be productive. When you finish your working day, go to a different part of your home and don't spend time in your work zone.

2. Take regular breaks. Many people neglect this when they're working from home but it's so important. Get up and move around. Personally, I take a five-minute break every 25 minutes, and I take a 15–20 minute break every two hours.

3. Build a routine. It's important to have structure to your day. Start and finish your working day at the same time as often as possible. Bundle your tasks throughout the day to help you structure your work. If emails distract you, agree to check them three times throughout the day, for example, but otherwise avoid your inbox.

4. Find a physical separator. What I mean by this is that you should have something that you do physically to separate your work from your home life. For a lot of people, getting dressed in 'work' clothes can really help.

5. Have a space where you won't be disturbed. If you are working from home with your family around, make sure they know when you shouldn't be disturbed. Have a quiet room that you can use for video calls and meetings. You could even make your own 'Do Not Disturb' sign to hang on the door. Turn off your email notifications during the day if you find these distract you too. Find a way of showing online that you shouldn't be disturbed.

6. Introduce online hours. Set hours when you will always be available online each day. Ideally, you need three to four hours each day where all the key members of the team are online at the same time, but manage this according to the time zones you are all in.

13

Building Power Communities

As Adam steps off the plane a wall of heat hits him. He knew it would be hot and humid here but wow. Suddenly, he feels hideously overdressed after the flight. He fights to remove his sweatshirt and feels relieved when he feels a slight breeze. He looks up at the clear blue sky and smiles. He's made it.

Although he's never met Paula in person before, he spots her instantly in the arrivals hall. Her curly hair is a dead giveaway, along with her beaming smile. She sees him emerging, bag in hand, and springs across to him. She hugs him warmly. 'Adam, it's so so nice to meet you properly!' He laughs. 'You too Paula.' She laughs too. 'I can't get over this! I'm so excited to show you all around my little corner of Brazil!'

They chat in the taxi all the way to the hotel. You would never know that they'd only met in person for the first time 15 minutes earlier. Paula leaves Adam to check in and get settled. The others are due to arrive over the coming hours.

After hitting the hotel gym, showering and changing, Adam goes down to the hotel bar. He's barely made it across the lobby when he hears someone call his name. He spins around to see Sunita and Maya waving at him. He hugs both of them. Sunita is smaller than he imagined. Paula is standing behind them, beaming. She laughs, the sound bouncing off the walls of the lobby. 'This is great!'

'I was just going to get a drink and some food,' Adam says. 'When are we expecting the others?'

'Jeff and Dave should both be here in a few hours,' Paula explains.

'Kaito isn't arriving until tonight,' Maya adds.

'Come and join me when you're ready ladies, I'll grab us a table – I'm starving.' Within half an hour, the four of them are happily chatting away. The alarm on Paula's phone suddenly starts going off. 'Airport time for me again!' she says brightly, flashing them all one more huge smile before leaving to get in a taxi.

She returns an hour later with both Jeff and Dave. Although Adam met Jeff at a conference years ago, he's taller than he remembered and he has an enviable Californian sun tan. Dave is looking relaxed after his week off to visit family in the US too.

'Great to have you both here!' Adam says. There are more hugs, more laughter and plenty more chatter as they all settle into one another's company. *Just Kaito to come.* Adam thinks.

Although they're all tired from their travels, they decide to wait up and greet Kaito before going to bed. His flight is due in at 10.30 p.m. Adam goes with Paula to the airport to meet him. 'You guys have been friends for a while right?' Paula asks.

'We met at an energy conference years ago. I knew no one and Kaito just happened to sit next to me in a lecture. One of the best contacts I ever made at a networking event!' Adam says with a broad grin.

When Kaito arrives and sees Adam waiting with Paula he smiles broadly. The two men embrace warmly before Paula wraps Kaito in a hug of her own. Adam hasn't seen the smile slip from her face all afternoon.

At the hotel everyone welcomes Kaito warmly and they happily talk before, eventually, going to bed. As they're getting up to go back to their respective rooms, Paula reveals she has a surprise planned, 'But not until tomorrow afternoon to give you all time to catch up on your sleep!' she says with a wink.

****

The following day, as instructed by Paula, the team gathers in the hotel lobby at 2 p.m. She's ready and waiting with a minibus outside. 'Are you really not going to tell us where we're going?' Adam asks with a laugh. 'Nope! Don't want to spoil the surprise,' she says, breaking into another of her infectious laughs.

On the drive through the streets of Salvador, Paula points out landmarks and talks about the history of the city. As they leave it behind they all fall silent, enjoying the tropical scenery rolling past the windows. After about an hour of driving, the minibus pulls over and they all disembark. Paula can barely contain her excitement as they each climb out.

Waiting for them at the top of the hill is a hot air balloon. 'Ta-daa!' she says. 'We're going to see our wind turbines in style!' The team are speechless. Adam turns to Paula, 'This is amazing, thank you.'

As they drift into the sky, there's plenty of nervous laughter with every little bump. Paula is conversing in rapid Portuguese with the balloon pilot, seemingly giving directions but Adam is sure he's seen her gesticulate like that in meetings too. After about half an hour of flying, everyone is feeling more comfortable when Kaito suddenly says, 'Look,' pointing to the south.

Just over the crest of a ridge of hills they can see the tops of the turbine blades. The balloon pilot takes them higher and gradually the wind turbines emerge from behind the tree line. There's hushed silence. Paula is the first to break it. 'I've been to visit the site before, but never like this,' she says. 'It's more beautiful than I could have imagined,' Sunita says beaming. They're staring in awe as the balloon starts to descend. A gust of wind knocks them to the side, wobbling the balloon and making them all grip the sides. They all start to laugh as the balloon steadies itself.

Slowly and gently, it lowers to the ground. One by one they climb out and stand looking up at the wind turbines that are now towering above them. As if from nowhere, the balloon pilot produces a hamper. 'Ah, perfect!' Paula opens it to reveal champagne and eight glasses.

'This seems as good a time as any for my speech,' Adam says with a laugh. 'I just wanted to take a moment to thank each of you for bringing us to this point. Kaito, thank you for supporting me from the start and for your confident and scientific approach to the development of this idea. Jeff, where would we be without your brilliant financial mind? I know I've also benefited from your sound advice on more than one occasion too. Sunita, you've brought so much passion as well as expertise to this team. Maya, I don't know how we managed in those early months without you, thank you for making all of our lives easier. Dave, it's been brilliant to continue to work with you and your input has been invaluable in so many ways. Last but not least, Paula, what can I say? Your playful character and contagious laughter has helped us through many an awkward meeting! And now here we all stand, next to the pilot of our wind project on the verge of an ICO. I couldn't be prouder of all that we've achieved so far and I know that with this team, we can achieve anything.'

He raised his glass to cheers and whoops from the rest of the group. As they stood watching the turbine blades slowly swoop around, Adam tuned into their surroundings. He could hear birds in the trees, feel the sun on his face and see a group of smiling faces. *Wow, we've done it. I can't wait to bring Georgia and Rose here one day. I've got a feeling that this is only the beginning…*

I've already mentioned several times about the importance of helping people in remote teams feel as though they're part of a community and in this chapter I'm going to take that one step further and talk about building power communities.

I'll share some lessons from two NGOs that I work with. At each I've helped them develop a global power team and then a global power community.

Case Study: Youth Against AIDS

Who Are They?

Youth Against AIDS is an NGO based in Germany that's fully driven and led by young people between the ages of 16 and 25. Some stay involved past this age, but that is broadly the range of people involved in the organisation. They have a management board of six people, then about 30 regional coordinators and approximately 3,000 volunteers.

Youth Against AIDS provides education in schools about sex and preventing the spread of AIDS. When I first engaged with them in 2014, they were running approximately 2,000 projects across Germany. Since then they've expanded, not only to run more projects but also to educate young people about other relevant topics.

How I Became Involved

I started working with them after they asked me to be the keynote speaker at their annual conference. Two years later, I went to Amsterdam to speak at their International Congress. Although Youth Against AIDS started in Germany, they have a global appeal and work with lots of African and Latin American colleagues who run similar NGOs in their countries.

I'd just like to tell you a brief story about my trip to Amsterdam for that International Congress, which illustrates why I do what I do.

I arrived late the night before the congress started, so I was already tired. After giving the keynote speech and a workshop on the same day, I was exhausted, I fell asleep on a train in Amsterdam. When I woke up, there was no one else on the train and all the doors were locked. The next morning, my family and I were supposed to be driving to Bulgaria for our summer holiday.

I called the emergency number on the train and after 40 minutes, a friendly Dutch man came to get me from the train. He unlocked the doors but he didn't let me get out. Instead, he got into the driver's seat and drove me, the only passenger on the train, to the main train station. When I got there, I realised I had missed all the decent connections to get home.

I managed to get as far as Bremen, where I then had a three-hour wait between 1 a.m. and 4 a.m. for my next train. I fell asleep on a bench in the station, only to be woken up by the police to check my identity! What a journey!

Why have I told you this story? Because if you asked me, even after this, whether it is all worth it: time away from my family, being tired, getting stuck at train stations, I would say a definitive yes!

Bringing people together, helping them unite and believe that they are more powerful as a team is an amazing feeling. I find it particularly rewarding when I get to work with social organisations that are working for a better world. I'm very grateful to have worked with a fantastic, purpose-driven organisation like Youth Against AIDS, as well as a number of other NGOs that I've helped over the years.

How I helped Youth Against AIDS

I worked with their management team, who all work free of charge for the NGO. They are the body that allocates the NGO's resources to ensure they're being used in the right way. They run initiatives, raise sponsorship and things like that. I ran a one-day workshop with them.

We quickly discovered there were two hot topics that we needed to resolve, and these are applicable to many NGOs. The two topics were focus and strategy.

In terms of their focus, they had a clear mission. They wanted to make every student in Germany aware of AIDS and how they can protect themselves from the illness. But they wanted to be more focused in their efforts. They felt that they lacked coordination sometimes, with too many events, initiatives and even PR going on. To achieve greater focus, you need more structure within an organisation.

What emerged from this workshop was that they needed to do more personal development. They were too young and didn't have any professional experience.

What We Did

Just as I explained at the beginning of the book, we applied the principles of the virtual power team to the leadership team in the NGO. We worked bottom-up to set goals, which, as you know, is an essential part of creating a virtual power team.

Each one of them took their sub-goals and milestones and really owned them. We also did some discovery about which of the skills they hadn't developed yet and we put together a development plan for each member of the leadership team. We discussed their strengths, as well as identifying the areas that needed more work.

We also did some work on the organisational structure. One of the keys here was to formalise their roles a little further. As an NGO, they're on a mission and everybody is doing everything. Each of the six members of the leadership team had their focus, so one was responsible for the finances, another for the media and marketing, another was the chair of the board, another dealt with the regional coordinators and so on. What we did was clarified these roles.

We introduced the concept that each role should have certain outcomes. It's not just about the activities that the people in these roles do, but about the outcomes they produce. We also clarified the key interfaces, because they needed to work with different people. Sometimes it was the geographical leaders, sometimes the functional leaders, other times it was external partners like political leaders who were supporting them, or sponsors, or media partners.

Another thing we did was identify ambassadors who would have a more external focus, which is key within an NGO. These people are the natural networkers and communicators. Within an NGO the key is to identify them and position them as ambassadors to maintain key relationships with the likes of sponsors, media partners, lobbyists and so on.

When we clarified the roles and the interfaces, they were able to visualise the organisational structure and see where they could strengthen communication. This exercise didn't focus as much on the individual as it did on the role itself, because there is turnover within the NGO, so this exercise was to give them more structure and allow them to more easily see who has the strengths to work well in each role.

I brought in my learning from the corporate world and we set up a matrix structure.

What was interesting was that as soon as they had this structure and had quantified the roles, they could see who would best fit each role to fulfill the desired outcomes. These decisions were based on the work they did through the strengths matrix. This chimed with my previous experience – that people volunteer for particular roles because they can see how they play to their strengths.

I find the strengths matrix particularly interesting because, over the years, I've observed that once you've done this exercise and you understand the importance of delegating according to people's strengths, you wonder how you could ever have worked in any other way.

Keeping Sight of the Big Picture

Also related to strategy was the concept of this big picture vision. As an NGO they had a vision, but we worked hard on establishing clarity of vision and focus. The reason this was so important was because they would sometimes lose their sense of progress because they had lost sight of that big picture.

Communicating this vision in a consistent way was also essential. At Youth Against AIDS they have social media and many interactive channels to communicate through.

I find that losing this sense of direction is relatively common in NGOs and the reason is that nobody helped them to formulate the big picture together. Of course there is a vision in an NGO, but more often than not this comes from the leader, rather than formulating it as a team. What I did was helped them to clarify their vision as a team. Then they all knew the big picture and could very clearly communicate that to others in the NGO.

Communicating Within the NGO

Another thing that we realised during this workshop was that there were many things happening in the regions, but there was not as much cooperation or knowledge-sharing as there could be. I talked them through some corporate case studies and they decided to introduce lots of regular updates.

These weren't just update meetings related to tasks or projects, but also personal updates, using the idea of sharing weekly highlights – what they had learned, what problems they were having and who they could ask for help.

Just by sharing these things, they found that they got a lot more support. This established a real sense of community when they were otherwise quite dispersed in a geographical sense.

Key Takeaways

Many organisations, both NGOs and businesses, still don't see the huge potential of strengths and, in particular, strengthening the strengths within the team. Once you discover and highlight people's strengths, they start to feel like heroes because they feel acknowledged for the extra skills and talents they bring to the table.

For NGOs, I would describe this as a key factor for unlocking their potential. But this is also true in a business environment, now more than ever with the transformation towards more remote work. Focusing on strengths will be key for the future.

Once you have a vision and build a strategic roadmap based around the topics that have the highest resonance for the team, you won't need to put people in roles. They will volunteer because they have a passion for the vision and with the roadmap you start breaking down the seemingly impossible into smaller, achievable milestones and goals.

The key to making the most of the strengths within your team is to do the preparation and lay the groundwork in an interactive format. If everyone is involved in this stage, they want to contribute to achieving the goals you set.

Lessons for a More Remote Future

Organisations of all sizes and types will need to find ways of creating virtual power teams in order to stay successful. In large corporates, they can sometimes be restricted by their own tradition or bureaucracy. When you use the strengths matrix there might be some blurring of boundaries, and big organisations with a traditional hierarchy will try to micromanage. This might work when they are all in the same office, even though it's far from optimal, but the more remote you go, the more you cannot micromanage.

The approaches that work in traditional hierarchies don't work in a remote work environment. NGOs don't have a boss or a bonus to motivate people, they only have empowerment and strengths and there is a lot that traditional organisations could learn from this, especially following the global Covid-19 pandemic. Becoming more remote and embracing these principles, sooner rather than later, will help them to survive.

Micromanagement doesn't work in a remote environment because you cannot control people in the same way. You can't look over their shoulder. The whole process of goal setting works within virtual power teams because those goals are interdependent and because people have chosen what they want to do and are therefore committed to doing their part in delivering as a team.

The difference in the level of motivation – when you have chosen what you're doing based on your strengths compared to being given a task to do – is huge. When you are working remotely, you don't have the same opportunities to be energised by your colleagues, so if you're given something to do that you didn't ask for, your level of motivation drops significantly.

Unless this task plays to your strengths, you will likely have more questions and therefore create unnecessary communication with your boss and your peers. You'll need to have more status update meetings to push you to deliver. All of a sudden, day by day, the negative effect on performance becomes greater.

The Importance of Frequent Updates

Having regular updates is something I discussed earlier in the book, but when I worked with Youth Against AIDS one thing we realised was that they didn't get together often enough to work on the project. The issues faced by the regional coordinators were very similar because they were facing the same challenges, just in different geographical locations, but they weren't sharing this with the others in the organisation.

What came out of creating a more sharing culture at the NGO was that often when someone had a problem, they could learn from someone else who had faced a similar problem.

Within Youth Against AIDS I encouraged them to have weekly updates to share any problems or challenges they were facing and to increase their levels of cooperation. But they also started including personal updates in these meetings. Previously, they'd just been getting straight down to business and they were missing the personal aspect of working as a team.

The regional coordinators would only meet once a year at the congress and then never meet again. So having these regular updates with their weekly highlights helped them bond a lot more as a team and that led to much greater cooperation. Unleashing this learning among the team members, and helping one another, boosted the success of their projects.

Regular Updates are Essential for Strengthening Bonds

Each member of a remote team is like a particle circling an atom, and if you don't have enough gravity then these particles get lost in space. Remote teams are the same, whether they are within NGOs or businesses, but it's particularly a problem for NGOs where they don't have a salary to at least start the bond.

This bonding is essential to strengthen the gravity within the team. But it's not only about bonding to each other, but also about bonding to the whole purpose.

Creating these bonds is also important when it comes to conflict management. If you want your team to be high performing, you can't avoid conflict. What you need is to resolve conflicts in a healthy way and to do that you need these bonds. When you are resolving a conflict, you need to distinguish between the problem and the individual. You need to be able to acknowledge that you may have different interests right now, but that you support and respect one another. The more political capital you have through bonding, the more successful your team will be at resolving conflicts in a healthy way and that's how they can reach their highest levels of performance.

If you don't have these strong bonds within your team, the conflict will escalate, sometimes to the point where it puts a whole project in danger. Even if not, there will be a lot of unnecessary communication around the conflict. People tend to email rather than just pick up the phone and talk it through. This all results in lower performance, not to mention making the work less fun for those involved.

Be Clear On Your 'Why'

As I said at the beginning of the book, you have to be clear on why you do what you do. In the NGO space, people are often attracted by the Why. It's the reason they joined the NGO in the first place. But that doesn't mean the Why can't be refined. Once you know the Why and you have got some people together, you need to drill down into personality. This is where the lifelines exercise comes in. It's about that personal discovery, then exploring people's strengths.

At the point that you add the 'Who' you may fine tune the Why a little. There will be an overall mission and the purpose of the team should be crystal clear. Then you can adjust the Why to play on everyone's strengths within the team.

You should start with your big Why, which is on the organisational level. Then there is the Why on the project level. As I discussed in Part 1, this is where you set SMART goals that lead to the interdependent goals for each team member and the strategic roadmaps that are based on people's strengths.

From an NGO's perspective, you need to constantly reiterate the big Why with the people on your team. This will help you navigate any challenges along the way. It will give your team the energy they need when they are faced with challenges. It helps them to be creative, to have resilience and to overcome those challenges. It will also show any stakeholders how you're succeeding with your vision, your Why.

When you're working remotely, the Why becomes even more important because you can't always lean on the shoulders of your teammates but you need to keep working towards your goal to have that impact.

Case Study: Teach For All

Who Are They?

Teach For All is another NGO. It started in America but it's a global organisation and I work with the Bulgarian branch. Their mission is to provide good quality education for every child, regardless of where he or she lives.

Often the teachers who get involved are on a mid-career sabbatical and they go and teach in underprivileged areas. In Bulgaria, there are about 50 regional coordinators and each one has approximately ten teachers to look after.

How I helped Teach For All

I ran a coaching session with the regional coordinators at the Bulgarian branch of the NGO. Out of this session they identified the challenges they were facing and their strategic roadmaps.

One of the key issues was that they seemed to be missing the big picture, even though they were all involved with the NGO because of its overarching purpose. The organisation had its big why but it wasn't translating this into terms the team could connect with. In Bulgaria, there are a lot of differences between schools and what was happening among the regional coordinators was that they were focusing on the differences and resolving each problem individually instead of looking for areas of commonality and sharing information.

What We Did

To encourage better information sharing, we introduced regular update meetings, in a similar way that we did with Youth Against AIDS. Similarly, Teach For All were also facing issues in terms of not bonding as a team.

Introducing the personal update, as discussed earlier in this chapter, helped to foster that sense of gravity in the team and set them on a positive upward spiral.

These regular updates also had another positive impact at Teach For All. They helped the organisation translate its big vision to the team. These regular updates were one of the big factors that unleashed them as an organisation.

Knowledge sharing was another issue that we worked on. As I said, the regional coordinators tended to focus on their differences, but they could be much more successful if they shared.

A lack of structure was preventing them from sharing, so I used all the Big Rocks of building a virtual power team to apply it to this community. People had passion for what they were doing, but there was low engagement, so we worked on defining roles, setting the goals bottom-up and creating SMART goals that were interdependent.

They also introduced a single source of truth for the mission and the key deliverables, which they previously hadn't had.

Bulgarians are very passionate, but they aren't always organised. In this case, there was sometimes not just duplicate but triplicate information, with many copies of the truth. There was also this lack of formality around roles that hindered creating and working from this single source of the truth.

Creating that single source was important to their future success. But, as with the Youth Against AIDS example, resolving these issues required a return to the basics of building virtual power teams: encouraging bonding, personal updates, knowledge sharing and showing vulnerability.

Empowerment and Trust Building

Now I'd like to share an insight into relationship building and trust. This comes from my toughest team, my family.

Like most teenagers, my three oldest daughters receive an allowance from my wife and me. They love to shop and they especially love to shop online. So, I made an agreement with them and gave them access to my PayPal account and I shared my password with them.

I can hear what you're thinking, 'Peter, you're a brave and crazy father!' Yes, I am, but I am also applying techniques to my toughest team that I have learned from working with virtual teams. The key drivers here are trust and relationship building.

When I showed them this trust, I could see the relationship strengthening and that has continued. Now the girls even go the extra mile. Often, before they buy something, they send my wife and I links of two or three examples of what they intend to buy and they discuss them with us.

I have never asked them to do this. If I had made this mandatory, they almost certainly wouldn't have done it. But because I show that I trust them, they take the initiative themselves.

Our mutual trust is deepened. They get what they want and I have a smooth-running team that is managing its budget carefully and consciously. I apply this same trust and relationship building to virtual teams.

Responding to Any Major Change or Disruption (Including A Pandemic!)

Globalisation and digital transformation have brought new challenges to leadership and communication. Businesses are often made and broken based on how they respond to unexpected major change or disruption, either within their industry or globally.

The Covid-19 pandemic provides an ideal case study for us to explore in relation to responding to any major change or disruption that is unexpected.

Case Study: The Covid-19 Pandemic

The Covid-19 pandemic has challenged us still further. Overnight, working from home became a necessity for millions of people around the world. Generally, we have responded well with strong personal commitment and good digital skills.

But it isn't enough for virtual teams to just function. As you will have gathered by now, they are capable of achieving so much more when the team is managed and run correctly.

The following are my insights into the global pandemic response, inspired by an article written by McKinsey[1]. Before I share my insights, I'll share the five key takeaways from the McKinsey article:

1. Gain a realistic view of your starting position.
2. Develop scenarios for multiple versions of your future.
3. Establish your posture and broad direction of travel.
4. Determine actions and strategic moves that are robust across scenarios.
5. Set trigger points that drive your organisation to act at the right time.

---

[1] https://www.mckinsey.com/business-functions/strategy-and-corporate-finance/our-insights/getting-ahead-of-the-next-stage-of-the-coronavirus-crisis?cid=other-eml-alt-mip-mck&hlkid=fa35dbc1a16543cdb7e41dea4d7ffdec&hctky=11862071&hdpid=50056e1f-1960-4ae3-b9a3-ff33b5ea692e April 2020

Their take is very strategic, whereas I've viewed what's happened through a more operational lens.

The Impact of Covid-19

The Covid-19 pandemic has delivered the biggest economic shock since World War II. Many businesses have failed as a result, many others have been put on hold, and some have profited significantly. But for the most part, Covid-19 has had a serious impact and not only economically. It has affected customer behaviours and resulted in businesses needing to rethink their business models.

How to Respond to the Unexpected

But how can you respond to the unexpected? I'll give you some advice on how you can 'plan' for such eventualities.

Set Up a Team

You need to be proactive and not just wait for events to happen to respond. I would advise setting up a team of the people with high potential in your company, the people who have demonstrated leadership potential and who are on a leadership development path. Set them a task to come up with various scenarios that might happen. Tell them to focus on uncertainty.

In the past when you did a strategy planning exercise you would make a couple of assumptions that you could be reasonably certain of, but now uncertainty is a very big player. It's the biggest elephant in the room, in fact, and you therefore need to plan several scenarios where, at this point in time, you're not sure what is more likely to happen.

To do this effectively, you need bright, specialist and committed people. This team also has to be cross-functional and it has to be diverse. By diversity I mean a mix of people of different ages, male and female, people of different nationalities. You're not only looking for your high potentials for this exercise, but a diverse mix of your high potentials.

When they come up with the scenarios, tell them to list very clearly the assumptions they are making for every one. For each scenario they should also come up with a plan over different time-scales. You need a short-term plan, for next week for example, a mid-term plan, for next quarter, and a long-term plan for one to two years.

This makes the exercise more complex, but this is what you need to do when you're trying to predict uncertainty on this scale.

Your high potentials need to go through these different scenarios based not only on different assumptions but also on different timescales. This is very different to traditional strategy planning, where you have greater certainty.

Research will be essential here. But they have an opportunity to do this very effectively with the level of intelligence and data that is being generated by what is happening in the market as a result of Covid-19. They need to look at what your competitors are doing. Don't forget to consider the possibility of coopetition. Could some of the scenarios make it logical for you to work with your competitors? If the market becomes so disrupted that you need to do this, what areas would be most successful? Perhaps R&D?

Accept the level of uncertainty in these strategies, confront it and gather as much data as possible for each of the scenarios and assumptions that you've made. Get this team to look at your annual business plan as well. They need to determine what their assumptions would mean for that business plan and your business model. How will it need to be updated under this new scenario? What new assumptions will you need to make? For each of the scenarios, you need to very clearly see the business outcomes.

How to Take a Tactical Approach

One of my first pieces of advice when approaching this exercise on a more tactical level is to look at what is common across your scenarios. While they may all be different, in some cases there may be a strong underlying factor or vision, which you can use to bring some certainty to the uncertainty.

Take Bill Gates as an example. In the early days of Microsoft, he wasn't sure which operating system would emerge, but his vision was that personal computing would be the next big thing.

Therefore, it would be a graphical interface. Based on that, he focused his attention on developing the next-level operating system knowing that personal computing was coming. You need to look for similar market signals in your industry. If there are any common trends then base at least some of your scenarios on that.

Never forget that the name of the game is uncertainty though. This isn't about having the best plan, because the plan will change. This is about being the best learner from the changing environment we find ourselves in.

This is why I shared that quote from John Lennon at the start of the book: 'A dream you dream alone is only a dream. A dream you dream together is a reality.'

Encourage your team to exchange ideas, draw conclusions and reflect together. Their aim should be to become the best adapter. As Darwin said, it is the most adaptable that survive and now we're living in a world where that's never been more true.

As a business, you need to be adaptable and therefore to plan in advance using your brightest minds to come up with scenarios to meet new challenges, face uncertainty and deliver business outcomes. This is how you will survive. Only the best adapters will come through such challenges and Covid-19 is just one example.

You also need to combine this learning with adapting on a bigger scale. You can't adapt in isolation. As well as your team of high potentials, you need others to come in and adapt their adjustments, make assumptions of their own and continue to challenge your thinking.

This is a lot of work, but remember that the fastest learners, those who are most successful at adapting, will be the ones who win in this fast-moving world. You always have to seek out the fastest improving trajectory.

The Road to Digitalisation

What we've seen, not just from the Covid-19 pandemic, but in general across business in the past decade, is that the more digital and automated you become, the more able you are able to cope with unexpected events.

Of course, not all companies have a digital product or service, but we've still seen that those who are most agile and adaptable, even in the physical world, fare better than those who aren't.

But the businesses that have experienced the lowest level of disruption as a result of the Covid-19 pandemic are digital companies. Some have even seen their businesses boom almost overnight. I'm talking about the likes of Zoom and Netflix that are completely digital and automated, and that have delivered solutions to the problems we have been facing.

Not every business can digitise. We still need to eat, get dressed and have physical products. But even if you have a physical product, it's time to look at your business process and where you can digitise and automate these. The quicker you follow the road to digitalisation, the more crisis-proof your business will become.

How digital and automated a company can become will vary from business to business and industry to industry, but what you need to do is decide what will work for you as an organisation and leverage the technology that helps your teams become more effective.

When you are carrying out the strategy planning exercise above, make one of the scenarios incredibly digitally focused and push it to be more digital than your current business model. Although it would be a major investment, consider new technology like artificial intelligence (AI) and how this could be introduced to your business.

Encourage your team to think about a much more digital way of performing business, including sales, marketing and some of the other essential processes that don't require a fundamental change to your main product.

Remember that you don't have to figure all of this out by yourself. One of the best things you could do is reach out to people outside of your organisation to get their thoughts. That might be your competition, or it could be an NGO with a similar purpose.

Whoever you reach out to, make sure that you find that common denominator with them on a purpose level. By that I mean why you do business, why are you doing what you do? If you broaden your scope in this way you could find many more partners. This will bring new perspectives and you can figure out these challenges together. I would strongly advise you to look to the world of NGOs, because they often think outside the box.

Leveraging Everyone in the Team to Promote Digitalisation

One of the key principles of the virtual power team is that you encourage everybody to contribute and leverage their strengths. When it comes to thinking about how to become more digital as an organisation, ideas can come from more places than your IT department.

We all use technology in our daily lives. Some of your team may even have a real passion for finding and exploring new technology. This is why it's so important to uncover the personalities of your team and discover their strengths. You might find people with a passion for digital in places you don't expect. They could be found in any department across your business.

This is also where you could come back to the concept of knowledge champions. Reach out internally and see who you have within your organisation who could help you find your path to greater digitalisation.

You may also want to consider reaching out externally. Could a brainstorming session with one or more of your competitors lead to some great ideas?

Career Visibility When Working Remotely

At the time of writing, we don't know how long people will be working from home as a result of the Covid-19 pandemic. While many European countries acted quickly and are relaxing their lockdowns after two to three months, the likes of the USA and Brazil are likely to see lockdowns lasting longer.

What I've seen during this period is people becoming afraid about how they will manage their careers and this is a question that I've been asked many times during virtual events in the months leading up to me writing this book. The common theme is that people feel stuck working from home and they want to know how to make themselves visible.

How it's best to make yourself visible during these times and when you are working remotely will depend on how your organisation works. If you are already part of a virtual power team, you will have full ownership of a goal. That means you'll have decision-making freedom, even if there are budgetary or time constraints.

Setting strategic goals bottom-up, building strategic road-maps and allowing people to pick their individual goals based on their strengths is the basis for empowering virtual power teams. If you have this, then you already have visibility. Having owner-ship of a goal goes hand in hand with the regular updates that are so important in virtual power teams, where you can report on where you are up to with your particular goal.

Of course, many people won't have this level of visibility because of bureaucracy, poor leadership and because they aren't given a way to report their progress. If you are facing this sce-nario, there are still things you can do and the most important is to be consistent.

You have to make sure somehow that you share your big why as an individual and communicate this clearly. To do this, you have to be clear about your purpose and what you stand for within the business. Make sure you regularly update people about this.

Within a virtual power team, we would use knowledge champions to share, collect and champion the knowledge which is relevant to the team and which matters to them. Normally these knowledge champions will be people with strength and expertise in a particular field.

If you don't have this kind of platform in your current organisation, then you have to find the right platform or tool within the corporate environment where you can share your knowledge and passion. Maybe there is an internal intranet where you can publish things.

The key is to deliver consistently on the purpose that you are standing for. Doing so will give you more exposure within the business. Within organisations that set up the basics correctly, this happens organically. All you have to do is live your passion. But this is not how your organisation works, you need to be proactive, make it clear what you stand for, find the right way to share your knowledge and consistently communicate.

Conclusion

Using the 10 Big Rocks to Foster Gravity

I've now introduced you to the 10 Big Rocks, broken down into three parts: the head, the muscles and skeleton, and the heart. But I'd like to bring you back to why it's so important to focus on all ten of these rocks to foster the gravity within your team.

Every one of these rocks is critical and they apply equally to local teams as they do to virtual teams. But when you have virtual teams, you cannot afford to neglect any of these ten big rocks. If you neglect one of them, you'll see the gravity among your team starting to loosen. Neglect a second one and it will become even looser. Neglect a third one and all of a sudden you'll start losing team members.

There are five key principles that you need to remember to create this strong and bonding team gravity:

- Promote personality: As I said at the start, you always need to start with your lifeline. When you have a new team member, make sure they present their lifeline using this holistic perspective. If you don't have time for the full exercise, ask the four magic questions. Use the personal update or weekly highlight to really promote personality in your regular team meetings. You need to present people as holistic humans, not just as experts.
- Empowerment: Do whatever you can to empower your team, such as with the interdependent goals and choosing their goal based on their strengths, after you have set the agenda as a team. Similarly, the optimal virtual culture is

not so hierarchical and should fall more on the egalitarian side of the spectrum. But again, the team should decide this depending on their culture. Use every opportunity to empower people and remember that micromanagement is not an option.

- Interdependent goals: Everyone should have their own strategic goal and these are interdependent. They should come out of the team vision, where you then identify the three key topics and then the roadmaps. You should formulate the goals from the roadmaps. In doing so, the team will take care of the performance. They will hold each other accountable, support each other and push each other when they need to because their goals are dependent on those of everyone else.

- Structured communications: Don't leave this to chance. Structure your communication in a way that everyone can contribute and shine. Don't allow the manager to dominate or point fingers.

- Winning spirit: Use an appealing prize for outstanding performance to encourage a winning spirit despite the distance.

When you focus on these key principles, and the 10 Big Rocks I've shared with you here, you'll create the optimal virtual power team culture, foster gravity between everyone on your team and enable them to perform at their very best.

Focus on Gravity

If you remember in the introduction to this book I talked about the *Apollo 13* mission and I'd like to bring you back to thinking about the universe for just a moment. Only 10% of the universe is material, things like planets and stars, 20% is nothing, black holes and other phenomena that scientists still can't explain. 70% is invisible energy like gravity that holds the universe together.

In a virtual power team, it's quite similar: 10% is the team members and infrastructure, 20% is the undeveloped potential, and 70% is the relationships, the trust and the gravity that holds these virtual teams together.

The art for leading virtual power teams is to focus on the 70% and I assure you that you'll be amazed by what you can achieve.

Epilogue

'd like to conclude with a sentence that has guided me through the years, and one that I shared with you at the start of this book.

'A dream you dream alone is only a dream. A dream you dream together is reality.'

Source: *The Playboy Interviews with John Lennon and Yōko Ono*, John Lennon, Yōko Ono, David Sheff Playboy Press, 1981.

The next time that Adam steps off a plane overseas, it's into the dry heat of the Sinai desert in Egypt and he has Georgia and Rose with him. Georgia can barely contain her excitement. She's spent most of the flight reading up on the marine life of the Red Sea.

Adam has treated them to a carbon-neutral diving holiday. He's paying to offset all the emissions they can't avoid and they have chosen a small, family-run dive centre and resort based in Dahab for their break. As their taxi winds its way through the dusky pink mountains that fringe Dahab, Adam begins to relax.

Their ten days will consist of a diving refresher for himself and Rose, while Georgia will be taking her first qualification. It's been a few years since they were able to go on a diving trip and Adam can't wait to feel the lightness of floating beneath the surface again.

He's also excited about diving with Georgia. He's sure she'll be a natural. One of the things that attracted them to this particular centre is that they offer reef ecology and conservation dives, where you can learn more about the underwater environment. They also run a weekly clean-up dive, which Georgia has, of course, insisted that they participate in.

He turns his head to see Georgia staring, wide-eyed, out of the window. The rugged mountains really are beautiful. As they turn a corner, the mountains part and, ahead of them, they can see the town of Dahab strung out along the coast, and the turquoise blue of the Red Sea.

****

On the third day of their holiday, Adam gives his phone a cursory glance. He's barely looking at it, confident that the team will handle everything in his absence. But there's a message from Maya. He's about to put his phone back on the nightstand and walk out of the hotel room when he has a change of heart. *I did only tell them to get in touch if it was something urgent.*

Maya is brief and to the point. Her message reads: 'Urgent: Peruvian government going 80% renewable energy. Want to work with us on the project.'

Adam reads the message twice, breaking into a broad grin. He even allows himself a fist pump. He replies: 'Set up the meeting ;-)' Then a second quick message: 'Make sure you invite Paula.' He wants her to take the lead on this one.

He sits on the edge of the bed, lost in thought. He remembers their two dives of the day, where the reefs were alive with colour, fish darting in and out of the corals. The intense blue of the ocean that seems to be bottomless. They even found an octopus sitting on a coral head. He'd spent a good five minutes observing it, watching as its colour shifted and it even changed the texture of its body to mimic the reef. *Nature really is incredible.*

He stirs from his thoughts and remembers why he came up to the room: to grab his wallet so they could go out for dinner. As they walk along the seafront with the calm blue waters of the Red Sea on one side and the mountains of Saudi Arabia turning a deep red across the gulf as the sun sets, Adam turns to look at Rose. Her face is beaming. He leans in and kisses her. She smiles. 'This has been wonderful.'

'I know, and I have some news that's going to make it more wonderful.'

'Oh?' Rose pauses, intrigued. Adam gently tugs her hand. 'I'll tell you both over dinner.'

Just as they start walking, Georgia swirls around to see where they are. She's radiant and bouncing. *Since her California trip she's become a real adult.* All of a sudden, Adam has a vision of her future, watching her get married, somewhere with the ocean in the background and dolphins dancing in the waves. *This is only the beginning.*

Index